FLOWER OF THE MOMENT

Gardeners' World

FLOWER OF THE MOMENT

Colette Foster

Editor

Louise Hampden

Horticultural Text

ILLUSTRATIONS
Page 2: *Lathyrus odoratus* 'Painted Lady'
Right: *Lilium regale*
Page 6: *Knautia macedonica*

This book is published to accompany the television series entitled *Gardeners' World*,
produced for BBC 2 by Catalyst Television Limited
Series producer: Colette Foster
Executive producer: Tony Laryea

Published by BBC Worldwide Limited
Woodlands
80 Wood Lane
London W12 0TT

First published 2001

ISBN 0 563 53414 1

Commissioning editor: Vivien Bowler
Project editor: Patricia Burgess
Adviser: Tony Lord
Art editor: Sarah Ponder
Designer: Sarah Jackson
Picture researchers: Bea Thomas, Miriam Hyman

Set in Perpetua and Trajan
Printed and bound in Great Britain by Butler & Tanner Limited, Frome and London
Colour separations by Radstock Reproductions Limited, Midsomer Norton
Jacket printed by Lawrence-Allen Limited, Weston-super-Mare

PICTURE CREDITS
The publisher would like to thank the following for their contributions to the book:
Peter Anderson 126; BBC Worldwide/Jo Whitworth 43; Jonathan Buckley 2, 4, 28,
29, 30, 38, 46, 58, 60, 63, 69, 71, 74, 75, 76, 77, 89, 91, 97, 100, 101, 102, 104,
106, 110, 111, 113, 115, 117, 119, 120, 121, 125, 127; Garden Matters 99, 114 left;
Garden Picture Library 25, 33, 59, 62, 72, 78, 80, 81, 98, 118, 131;
Stephen Hamilton 129; Jerry Harpur 10 left, 16, 17, 18, 19, 26, 27, 44, 49, 57, 65,
67, 85, 86, 94, 95, 128; Marcus Harpur 6, 8, 15, 23, 31, 47, 70, 84, 87, 88, 90, 93;
Clive Nichols 13, 14, 20, 24, 32, 35, 36, 37, 39, 40, 41, 42, 51, 52, 53, 55, 56, 64,
68, 71 left, 73, 79, 83, 92, 103, 105, 107, 109, 112, 114 right, 122, 123;
William Shaw 11, 54; Harry Smith Collection 45, 50

CONTENTS

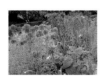

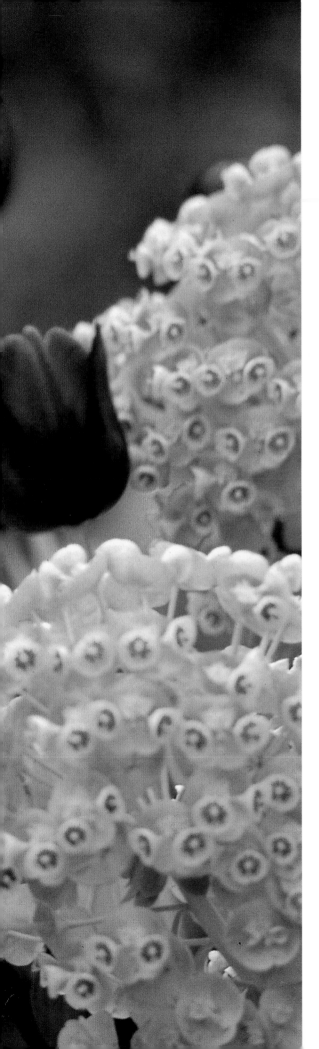

INTRODUCTION

When I started gardening as a child, the pictures on the seed packets I bought in Woolworth's sparked off dreams of the wonderful flowers that would emerge from the sprinkled contents. Alyssum was one of the first things I sowed, but at the age of nine what I had not yet understood was the relative scale of the plants. I thought they would all be as big as hydrangeas. Go on, take a look at an alyssum plant and magnify it to the power of a hundred. It's a hydrangea. But the flowers, though small, had a far better fragrance than the hydrangeas that grew in the corner of the garden, so my eyes were opened to the tremendous variety available in plants and flowers – some were large and some small, some were fragrant and others downright smelly – but they all engaged my interest.

Next came some young dahlia plants bought from a local nurseryman, and I looked forward to the spiky 'cactus' flowers I would cut in late summer. I bought my plants in early May. In Yorkshire you don't plant out dahlias until the end of May or early June, and so, with the nurseryman's warning about their frost tenderness ringing in my ears, they stood for the next four weeks in the hall on a shelf above the night storage heater. Another lesson learned: they were 2ft tall come planting time, but they still gave their all in August and September. Happy memories.

Since then I have never stopped learning about flowers. My entire year is marked out by the flowering time of so many of the plants included in this book. When asked what is my favourite flower, I always say that it depends on the time of year. In January, it has to be snowdrops – the first sign that the garden is coming back to life after the worst the winter has thrown at it. Then come daffodils. In my youth I believed the bigger, the better – 'King Alfred' or nothing – but now dwarf narcissi are my preference, small but perfectly formed, and they don't fall over in the rain.

Tulips follow – they don't come more dark and mysterious than 'Queen of Night', but I always prefer to grow them in pots and shift

Tulipa 'Queen of Night' and *Euphorbia characias*

Kniphofia 'Little Maid'

them out of the way once their flowers have gone so that no messy foliage hangs around upsetting the border. And by then I'm ready for the roses. What torture! It would be impossible for me to choose just one favourite, but in *Rosa* 'Geranium' there are two seasons of interest – a shock of bright red flowers in June and sumptuous, flagon-shaped rosehips later in October. Two for the price of one.

So some plants remind me of childhood, and others are dates for my diary. But there are also mementoes of happy occasions and meetings with great gardeners, some of them local, others more renowned. The Duchess of Devonshire grows grey-leaved verbascums in a pavement of gravel at Chatsworth House in Derbyshire. The six she gave me ten years ago I also planted in gravelly soil at Barleywood, and now dozens of their descendants have seeded themselves all over the garden, popping up somewhere different each year.

You see, gardens don't just change by the season or the month – a flower can have a short time in one part of the garden but may never be seen there again. Cherish the moment. A gift of erythroniums from Beth Chatto, the doyenne of British gardeners, flowers in my woodland garden each April, while spires of *Verbena bonariensis* remind me of visiting Christopher Lloyd at Great Dixter: he gave them to me long before their currently fashionable status made them all the rage.

Not all my plants come from such notable gardeners, and nostalgia plays a big part in the flowers I choose to grow. My grandfather loved wallflowers and garden pinks, both of which grew in the borders alongside the path that led to the front door of his house. But it is sweet peas that remind me most of him. I have a photo of myself – aged about a year – with grandad in his black trilby, black waistcoat and rolled-up sleeves, leading me through the towering plants on his allotment. I can't sniff them now without remembering him.

What does 'Flower of the Moment' mean? It always amazes me that gardening has become trendy, that the garden is now an outdoor room and that no surface of the garden has been spared the scrutiny of the style police. Yet perhaps too little attention is paid to what actually gets planted. 'Flower of the Moment' is not about the fashionable status of the plants; it's a timely reminder that should put your mind at ease.

The aim of this book is to take the mystery out of what is sometimes seen as the tricky bit, yet there is no reason for anyone to be put off by gardening jargon and technical grow-how. And if at first you don't succeed…well, you can always go and buy another plant. Gardening should be uplifting, not disheartening – there are plenty of things in the world far more worrying than a dusting of mildew on roses or clematis wilt. We've also chosen plants that shouldn't suffer too much at the hands of the British weather, so there is maximum enjoyment potential for every month of the year.

The members of the team who work with me on *Gardeners' World* have an unrivalled horticultural knowledge, and one of the great things about working with them is that they are in touch with the latest developments in the gardening world. Louise Hampden is our horticultural backbone. No plant gets on to the programme before Louise has scrutinized it, checked the footage and double-checked that the plant we are featuring is given the correct name. This is all part of the process of supplying viewers with the exceptional horti-cultural expertise that they have come to expect of the programme.

The series producer, Colette Foster, has her eye on the big picture, ensuring that detailed horticultural information is entwined with stunning pictures of gorgeous plants. She makes sure, too, that the passionate individuals who grow the plants also get their say – the *Gardeners' World* team is forever speaking to nurserymen, growers, professionals and amateurs – and we're grateful to them all for their time, expertise and enthusiasm.

Geranium 'Rozanne'

'Flower of the Moment' makes a simple yet vital point – that nature has an infinite number of ways of satisfying the gardener in all of us, whatever the time of year.

There's no rush to do it, but ultimately, I promise, you will want to have all these plants in your garden. Our favourite 100 are here in full bloom, but there is also an invaluable 'calendar' at the back of the book, listing 1000 flowering plants and showing their high season of spectacle, their colour, preferred growing conditions and size.

Whether you are starting from scratch and making your first visit to a garden centre or nursery, or searching for *the* plant to grow from seed that will complete your border, this is the perfect book from which to make your selection. Here you will find a collection of plants worth more than a moment of your time.

Enjoy them.

Alan Titchmarsh

MARCH

In March, plants from late winter continue to set the scene for chilly days, but a few more are brave enough to join the spring garden. There is a rush of activity as fleshy buds and translucent shafts of young leaf force their way to the surface, but flowers can be scarce.

At this time of year we get a little impatient on *Gardeners' World* since the choice for filming appears very limited. This concentrates our minds on what is valuable in the March garden, and ground-cover plants must be close to the top of everyone's list. Although their flowers are few, these are the first to replace the brown soil of winter with the colour of spring, and this is reflected in our choice.

March is often the month when new gardeners graduate from make-over programmes to *Gardeners' World*, and this is where 'Flower of the Moment' comes in. It provides guidance on how to care for plants you may already have, and suggests new ones that make precious additions to the spring garden.

Getting to know a plant's habit, where it likes to be grown and what can be done with it in the future are all part of the gardening cycle that we feel you would like to know. Since one plant has the potential to last a lifetime, there is also guidance on simple propagation methods.

We also enjoy discovering the history of each plant, in some cases researching little-known facts that may not have been presented before, and that too has influenced our choice of plants. This means that alongside the therapy of getting your hands dirty, you can also have the pleasure of getting to know your garden plants in a new way.

Anemone blanda The shrivelled appearance of *Anemone blanda* tubers gives no hint of the delights to come, for with the first signs of spring they burst forth with fresh-faced, daisy-type flowers in pale blue, mauve, pink or white.

• The 'enchanting windflower', as its name translates, grows in rocky, open places in the eastern Mediterranean, but adapts happily to domestic conditions on sunny banks, in rock gardens, in partially shaded places under shrubs and even in containers. Growing to just 10 cm high, *A. blanda* will return year after year once it has settled, carpeting the ground most effectively.

• Among the brightly coloured varieties are 'Radar', which is magenta pink with a white centre, 'Charmer', which is a deep rose pink, and 'White Splendour', which is pure white. Also worth looking out for is 'Ingramii', which naturalizes into drifts of an intense deep blue, carpeting the ground with dark green, lobed leaves. These are followed quickly by numerous erect stems bearing star-shaped flowers, which have bright yellow stamens at their centre.

• Tubers need to be soaked in warm water before planting, but take care not to leave them longer than 24 hours. Plant them in the autumn about 5 cm deep and 5 cm apart, and use at least 10 tubers to form a drift. This acts as an insurance policy in case some tubers don't come up, but it is also good planting practice, as a lone anemone plant is never going to look good.

• The woodland native *A. nemorosa* is another worthwhile plant that grows from rhizomes. This one likes to be planted in shade and produces simple flowers, having only 6–8 petals. The variety 'Robinsoniana' is early flowering, with wisteria-blue flowers and rounded petals.

Chionodoxa luciliae Chionodoxas are among the first bulbs to
flower in the spring, following hard on the heels of the snowdrop.
Their native habitat is the stony hillsides of Turkey, where they flower
amid the receding snows of winter, but they will grow in either sun
or partial shade, seeding about and eventually forming a colony.

• Chionodoxas grow only 15 cm high,
but make lovely drifts of white, pink
or blue under trees, shrubs or roses.
Flowering lasts for 3–4 weeks, after
which the flowers and foliage fade
from sight.

• *Chionodoxa luciliae* produces a mass
of bright blue, star-shaped flowers
over the small, strappy leaves, each
six-petalled flower radiating out from
orange stamens and fading to white at
the centre. C. 'Blue Giant' is larger and
flowers at the same time, and C. 'Pink
Giant' makes lots of impact with several

soft violet flowers to the stem. The
strongest blue of all is *C. sardensis*, a deep
gentian colour.

• Chionodoxas are so obliging that they
can be planted in rock gardens in the sun
or in pots in an alpine house, where the
tiny flowers can be closely appreciated,
but they must be grown *en masse* to get
the full 'sea of blue' effect. Plant them
liberally in fertile soil with plenty of grit
added for drainage, burying the bulbs
8 cm deep. Pot-grown bulbs have similar
soil requirements. To show them off to
best advantage, add a dressing of grit.

'One plant has
the potential to
last a lifetime'

Caltha palustris This hardy perennial, also known as the marsh marigold or kingcup, is common throughout the cold and temperate regions of the northern hemisphere. Among the most beautiful of British wild plants, it flowers very early in the spring in marshes or by the edges of streams and ditches.

• Its waxy, golden flowers, measuring about 2.5 cm across, appear above deep green, kidney-shaped leaves, which root where they touch the soil and form a spreading clump.

• The variety 'Flore Pleno' is one of the showiest of March plants and has been cultivated in gardens since the seventeenth century. It blooms generously from March to June, and a second crop of flowers can appear in September and October.

• Marsh marigolds will grow in water to a depth of 20 cm, as well as in bog gardens and sunny areas that remain continuously moist. Their clumps of glossy foliage look good in marginal plantings with the leaves of *Iris pseudacorus* and, for an even lusher effect, with rodgersias and ligularias.

• Overcrowded plants can be easily lifted and divided in the autumn, giving replanted clumps time to re-establish before their early spring flowering.

Epimedium × *warleyense* Epimediums are useful ground-covering plants found growing wild across the whole of Asia. Most varieties are evergreen, and if planted in partial shade in compost-enriched soil, they will slowly grow to form a mat of glossy, dark green, heart-shaped leaves.

• It is the foliage that requires a 'hands-on' approach. From March onwards the leafless flowering stems start to appear from the ground under the leaves, and it is then that swift action is needed with a pair of shears. Clipping over the plant and removing the crispy leaves gives the flowers a chance to show themselves off, as they emerge in great numbers on wiry stems.

• *Epimedium* × *perralchicum* has numerous, orange and yellow flowers sprouting along the stems, which create a lovely airy effect if grown *en masse*. Fresh new foliage takes over the display, starting life pale green with bronze-red marbling from the margins inwards, then gradually becoming dark, glossy green during the late spring and summer. In some varieties the foliage takes on bronze and copper tints with the onset of autumn.

• Once established, epimediums will obligingly cover the ground, suppressing all weeds. They make excellent edging plants alongside a shady path, being tough and tolerant of the occasional tread by an errant foot.

• Increasing plants is easy: simply lift and divide the rootstock into smaller pieces and replant in the autumn. New plants will take a year before they are mature enough to start flowering again.

Epimedium **is the Latin word for 'bishop's mitre', the shape of which perfectly parallels the flower shape of the elegant woodland plant named after it.**

Pulmonaria 'Sissinghurst White' Ground-covering but
never invasive, the pulmonaria has spotted and slug-proof leaves,
and a delightful flowering habit, which give it year-round value
in the garden. It also makes a great foil for early spring bulbs or
hellebores in shady places.

• 'Sissinghurst White' is one of the most
beautiful varieties of pulmonaria. Easy to
grow, vigorous and with strong leaf
markings, it is an asset under shrubs and
trees, and the flowers, although small,
make a dazzling haze of colour at a difficult time of year.

• Pulmonarias have a lovely habit of
seeding themselves around, and although
the colour and form will not come true,
it can be interesting to see what appears.
After flowering is a good time to remove
old leaves, which will quickly be replaced

by fresh foliage. Purists like to dead-
head their plants.

• As summer progresses and the soil
becomes drier, the leaves can get
covered in mildew, but this is soon
remedied by cutting the plant back
because new and fresh foliage will
quickly form. Giving it partial shade and
a good mulching will act as preventive
measures. More plants can easily be
made by dividing the clump into smaller
chunks. Make sure you get rid of any
blackened roots at the same time.

Bergenia 'Bressingham White' The large leaves of evergreen bergenias have given rise to the plant's common name, elephant's ears. Up to 25 cm across, they add form and colour to the spring garden, turning to rich shades of mahogany and red over the winter if they are planted to catch the sun. Being tough plants, bergenias make extremely good ground cover that will suppress any weeds, and can be left for years without any attention. Provided they have a well-drained soil, they are not fussy about their location, enjoying shade as well as sunny conditions.

• The flowers are produced on stout, reddish stems, and can be in varying shades of pink and white. The many individual little bells that make up the flower-head of 'Bressingham White' are pure white and long-lasting. Spent flower-heads and damaged leaves should be cut off from the base once flowering has finished to make way for the fresh, young, shiny leaves that will clothe the plant throughout the summer and into the winter.

• Bergenias grow from tough rhizomes, which, in established clumps, become very visible on top of the soil. As soon as these rhizomes create a vast network, leaf and flower formation is reduced, and that is the time for renewal. You can be tough with the clumps: take a knife to them in spring and chop them up, making the cuts at leaf-growing points. The new 'chunks' can be replanted immediately, and will quickly grow to cover 30 cm of ground.

' Getting to know a plant's habit is part of the gardening cycle '

Muscari armeniacum Reliable and undemanding, muscari bulbs last for years, quietly increasing with every season. *Muscari armeniacum* is the species most often planted. The chive-like leaves appear months before the flowers, and, where bulbs are densely packed, they can make a thick and weed-suppressing carpet. From the centre of each individual spray of leaves the developing flower becomes increasingly visible, gradually growing into a spike from which tightly clustered, tiny blue bells open, each with a pursed mouth. Their common name, grape hyacinth, derives from their resemblance to an inverted bunch of grapes.

• Although a native of southern Europe, and therefore a sun-lover, *M. armeniacum* also grows well in northern Europe, particularly on sunny banks, but also in rock gardens and at the front of borders. Large spaces look wonderful if bulbs are mass-planted in a river-like shape. The foliage dies down completely over the summer, so to avoid a gap, plant carpets of them with early narcissi among perennials that will take over the space.

• Other good varieties of muscari are 'Blue Spike', with scented, double, showy and long-lasting spikes, 'Valerie Finnis', in a delicate pale blue that looks good in pots, and the white variety *M. botryoides* 'Album', which has the added advantages of unfloppy leaf stems shorter than the flower, a good clump-forming habit and fragrance.

Muscari comes from the Greek word *moschos*, meaning 'musk'. The flowers of some species do have a slight fragrance, which is best enjoyed indoors from blooms that have been pulled rather than picked.

APRIL

Longer evenings, gently warming sunshine, feathery foliage and subtle scent set the scene for the April garden. The chemistry that creates a **surge** of new growth to replenish our gardens will soon cause plants to compete for our attention.

If you have left plants to add structure to the winter garden, it's a time to be brave and take the shears to them to make way for all this **activity**. If it's a busy time for plant life, it is most certainly a busy time for gardeners, but there are good reasons to be out there.

Spring is epitomized by carpets of daffodils, while scent wafts at nose height with *Clematis armandii*. The summer canopies of trees are yet to open, so woodland flowers, such as the **delicate** *Corydalis flexuosa*, sparkle in low light, while *Euphorbia griffithii* 'Dixter' soaks up the early sun. In short, there are now plants for all situations.

Gardeners can also do their bit to conserve endangered flowers. Many that are becoming rare in their natural habitats, such as *Fritillaria meleagris*, will **thrive** in gardens if given the right conditions. Wherever possible, we have taken the myth and mystery out of growing plants, and while keen gardeners start from seeds and cuttings, this is the perfect time to garden an easier way.

We would always recommend autumn planting so that a plant has time to settle in before its new season's **growth**, but if that season has been particularly wet, pot-grown plants bought in spring are the next best alternative. These can be bought from specialist nurseries and garden centres, or delivered straight to your door by mail order or the Internet. Get them straight into the ground for instant displays. This approach is a little more expensive, but a small price to pay when divided by the subsequent years of **pleasure**.

Corydalis flexuosa 'Père David' Introduced from China at the end of the 1980s, *Corydalis flexuosa* is a small plant, covering an area of 20 cm and reaching 30 cm high in a short growing season. All trace of the plant disappears during the summer months, then fresh foliage appears in the autumn in time to give winter interest to the garden.

• The delicate, slender and spurred flowers of *Corydalis flexuosa* appear to hover over their light green, ferny foliage in flights of vivid turquoise or opalescent blue, which can light up the gloom of a shady space. Their delicacy can give the impression that they are difficult to grow, but Corydalis are surprisingly easy as long as three requirements are satisfied: dappled shade, leafy, gritty soil and a position in the garden that is not too dry.

• There are several cultivars: 'Père David', with dark azure flowers; 'Purple Leaf', with sky-blue flowers over bronze foliage; and 'China Blue', which speaks for itself. Pale yellow primroses and the golden leaves of *Carex elata* 'Aurea' make good partners in the dappled shade of a woodland planting.

• Corydalis rapidly lose their vigour, so divide them regularly to keep them robust and flowering well. This is easy to do in early autumn by digging up the roots, pulling them into small pieces and replanting them immediately. (Remember to keep them moist if there is a lack of autumn rain.) Corydalis also flourish in pots, but the containers must be given a shady position throughout the year.

> Spring is a busy time for plant life, and most certainly a busy time for gardeners

Trillium grandiflorum Trilliums are often, but erroneously, thought to be difficult plants to grow; as a result, they are not grown enough. Give them the right conditions and these spectacular spring plants will thrive.

• The fleshy, rhizomatous roots love to be deep in moist, leafy soil in full or partial shade. Grow them in neutral or acid soil and dig in lots of composted bark or leaf mould before planting, allowing plenty of space to give the roots the moisture and nutrients they need. Trilliums do not like disturbance or lots of competition from neighbouring plants, as they like to spread.

• Almost as beautiful in bud as in flower, *Trillium grandiflorum* is one of the hardiest species, with buds pointing upwards over its ruff of leaves before opening to a dazzling white that gradually fades to a pink flush as it ages.
• *T. luteum* has an added bonus of marbled leaves under the lemon to butter-yellow flowers, while *T. sessile* has bronze-marked leaves and flowers of deep maroon.

• The foliage of trilliums dies down in the summer, when clumps can be divided and replanted; alternatively, seed can be collected and sown in the autumn. Good companion plants are the nodding, yellow *Uvularia grandiflora*, which will flower at the same time, and hostas, which mature much later and whose leaves will cover the ground during the trilliums' dormancy.

Erythronium californicum 'White Beauty' Erythroniums are commonly known as dog's tooth violets because the bulbs are shaped like fangs. They are native to meadows and damp woods in Europe, Asia and North America, and one of the best varieties is 'White Beauty', which comes from northern California. Its exquisite lily-shaped and creamy-white flowers open above shiny, two-toned leaves, and the swept-back petals reveal long stamens and rusty-red markings at the base.

• Given dappled shade and soil improved with lots of leaf mould that is not allowed to dry out, erythroniums will grow vigorously to 20 cm tall. Their clumps can be left to naturalize, or be divided after flowering, before the plant dies down for the rest of the year.

• Bulbs should be planted (pointed end up) in the autumn at a depth and distance of 10–12 cm. Don't leave your bulbs in the bags where they can dry out: plant them as fresh as possible. Then sit back and wait for some spring-time colour.

Erythronium californicum 'White Beauty'

Narcissus 'Thalia' There is an overwhelming choice of narcissi, from the tiny *Narcissus cyclamineus* to the huge trumpets of 'King Alfred'. With careful selection, it is possible to have daffodils in flower in the garden from late January through to the end of May.

• For elegance and perfume in the April garden our choice is N. 'Thalia'. The flowers of this variety are pure white, delicate and slender, 5 cm wide and angled towards the ground. Their petals flare back from the central cup.

• Narcissi will tolerate sun and a bit of shade provided the soil is well drained but moist during the growing period. 'Thalia' has a preference for warm, sunny places, and, being just 30 cm tall, is frequently used in rock gardens.

• The most important time for narcissi bulbs is after flowering, when they gain strength from the light and sun on the plant's leaves to build up the bulb for next year's flower. Snap off any spent flowers, feed with a general-purpose fertilizer and leave them alone for six weeks: the leaves will soon die away. Alternatively, grow daffodils in pots and plunge them into borders when in flower. Once over, move them to a place where they can't be seen to die down.

Sometimes bulbs do not flower at all, and there are two principal reasons for this. Either they have built up so well that they are over-crowded, or they have not been planted deeply enough. In both cases, lift and split the clumps while the leaves are still visible, and replant them at two and a half times the depth of the bulb.

Euphorbia griffithii 'Dixter'   There is a euphorbia for almost every situation in the garden, but it's no surprise that 'Dixter' is so popular. Its flame-red bracts and young leaves in coral red make a striking show when grown in groups in a sunny spot. This plant provides interest from April right through to September, holding on to its bracts for weeks and giving the added bonus of autumn foliage colour. It likes a moisture-retentive soil, where the rhizomes will spread but not take over, allowing bulbs to be planted in between.

• If you have a large space to fill, the shrub-like structure and early flowering habit of *Euphorbia characias* is ideal. For smaller spaces *E. dulcis* 'Chameleon' has a dwarf habit, but seeds freely and has unusual dark purple leaves. In a warm spot with plenty of drainage the tender *E. mellifera* will act as a magnet to bees when in flower and waft a delicious fragrance over the garden.

• The flowering bracts of euphorbias need to be cut down every year, usually in June, but take care: their sap is an irritant, so always wear gloves when handling them. Cutting back gives strength to the new foliage sprouting from the base rather than helping seed production. This makes sense because many varieties produce seedlings that may not be as good as their parents.

Euphorbias were named after a first-century Greek physician called Euphorbus. He used their milky sap for medicinal purposes.

Primula vulgaris The appearance of the common primrose signals the end of winter, and this can happen any time from the end of February onwards. Its main and most prolific flush of flowers is in April, but certain other primulas will flower well into July.

• The common primrose grows in the wild along grassy banks, in ditches and at the foot of hedgerows, for it thrives in light shade and heavier soils. The lemon yellow or cream flowers obligingly seed around, moving themselves into fresh soil and different positions.

• All primulas suffer from replant disease and will die if constantly replanted in the same spot year after year. Naturalized plants avoid this through their seeding habit, but in gardens they must be divided regularly and moved somewhere completely different to keep them strong and healthy. The best time to do this is in May, which is also the best time to collect and sow fresh seed.

• If you would like a change from the usual shades of yellow and cream, try some of the enchanting old varieties. 'Lilacina Plena' has double flowers of pure lilac, while 'Wanda', a cottage garden favourite, grows in a wonderfully vivid claret colour.

Clematis armandii

Evergreen, scented, climbing and spring-flowering, *Clematis armandii* is on the wish list of most gardeners. Found by the plant hunter Ernest Wilson, and brought from China in 1900, this plant needs a bit of careful nurturing.

• In a happy location, on a south- or southwest-facing wall, it is rampageous, reaching heights of 4.5 m and over. Its large, dark green and glossy leaves, which are bronze when young, mature to a leathery texture. As an evergreen, *C. armandii* flowers on growth made in the previous year, so it is essential to place it in a sheltered spot as severe weather can cause damage, resulting in the loss of flowers. Any pruning should be carried out after flowering, giving new growth time to mature over the summer to carry next year's flowers.

• Flowering is profuse. The pure white blooms, 4–5 cm in diameter, have five or six petals surrounding off-white anthers on short stems. Clouds of these flowers will emit a powerful fragrance on a warm spring day. The variety 'Apple Blossom' has pale pink flowers scented strongly of vanilla.

• *C. armandii* needs moisture and well-drained soil – not the usual conditions found against warm brick walls. The solution is to dig a deep planting hole at least 30 cm away from the wall and fill it with good compost and well-rotted manure. This will help to retain moisture, as will a top-dressing of gravel. A mulch of manure in the autumn will nourish the plant.

Pulsatilla vulgaris Pulsatillas are stunning plants. The leaves are ferny, catching the morning dew, while the stems and flower-buds are covered in gossamer-fine hairs. The flowers open out into chalice shapes of lavender blue to deep purple, and the stamens are deep gold.

- Although native to the chalk downs and meadows of northern Europe, pulsatillas will thrive in most soils as long as they are well drained, get plenty of moisture in the spring and have full sun. Being only 30 cm in height and spread, they are ideal in rockeries.
- *Pulsatilla vulgaris* var. *rubra* stands out, its golden stamens contrasting with its bright red petals, while *P. vulgaris* 'Alba' has white flowers that shimmer against its coating of silvery hairs. Dead-heading helps to prolong the flowering period, but stop towards the end so that the seed-heads remain to be enjoyed.
- Seedlings are available in early autumn, or plants can be bought in flower from garden centres in spring. They should be planted out with extra grit and compost added to the planting hole.
- Once flowering has finished, the seed-heads gradually ripen and fill with long, luxuriant bristles, which can be collected and sown immediately. Plants can also be divided after flowering, or root cuttings taken during their late autumn dormancy.

Fritillaria meleagris   There are over 100 species of fritillaria found in the northern hemisphere, but only a limited number are cultivated. The native *Fritillaria meleagris*, commonly known as the snake's head fritillary, has nodding bells on top of wiry stems, and leaves that are no thicker than a blade of grass. The water meadows where they are naturalized have damp soil but good drainage for most of the year, and it is these conditions under which they will thrive in the garden.

- The hanging flowers are usually red, but these are overmarked in white, pink and purple with patterns that resemble a chequer board or the mottled skin of a snake. Pure white forms appear in the wild in about 10 per cent of seedlings; these can be purchased under the name *alba*.
- The snake's head fritillary can easily be naturalized in the garden in a damp patch of grass in either sun or dappled shade by scattering handfuls of the tiny bulbs around and planting them where they fall, making sure they are buried to a depth of about 5 cm. After flowering the grass must remain uncut for at least six weeks to allow the fritillaries to ripen their seeds and let them fall. Above all, avoid any fertilizers, as these will encourage coarse grass to grow and eventually choke out the fritillaries.

A surge of new growth replenishes our gardens

Brunnera macrophylla There is always room in every garden for a 'tough as old boots' plant, a workhorse that can be planted in unpromising places and left alone to get on with it. *Brunnera macrophylla* is indispensable in the dry conditions found under evergreen shrubs or trees, and quickly forms a weed-suppressing mat of round, rough-textured leaves. In fact, shade is ideal for brunneras, as their broad leaves can be scorched by cold winds and too much sunlight.

• After the leaves have covered the ground, delicate sprays of intense blue, forget-me-not-type flowers appear, and last for weeks until the onset of summer. Brunneras will set seed and grow away into fresh plants that may need weeding out if they are in the wrong place, but early dead-heading will prevent this.

• 'Hadspen Cream' is a lovely variety, which has pale green leaves with creamy variegation. This variety must have its roots divided to make new plants.

• Brunneras are virtually maintenance-free, but clumps can be rejuvenated for the summer if the whole plant is sheared to the ground. Fresh foliage will soon sprout up along with an occasional show of late flowers.

MAY

The garden gets into full swing in May, and the range of colours, shapes, textures and foliage expands to create some **divine** planting schemes in both sun and shade.

Many May flowers are woodland plants and therefore perfect for shady gardens – the sort we are most often asked about on *Gardeners' World*. There is an enviable plant selection to choose from if your garden is **shady**. Understanding the right growing conditions can also be the key to planting combinations. If the damp woodland floor is the **natural** home of aquilegias, dicentras, *Convallaria majalis* and *Geranium phaeum*, they will look good planted alongside each other. The shade of an emerging tree canopy will also protect them from the full glare of summer sunshine.

The lengthening daylight hours and intensity of the sun's heat make way for some real **sun-lovers** too. Poppies and peonies, for example, bring touches of the Mediterranean to the temporarily sun-drenched spots of Britain.

Later in the year, many May flowers also provide a wholesome harvest, and the seeds of poppies, nigellas and aquilegias can be collected or left to scatter themselves. This is one of the cheapest yet most **rewarding** forms of gardening, providing successive years of enjoyment from just a handful of well-placed seed.

Entire books have been written about many of the plants we are featuring, and we cannot expect everyone to agree with our disciplined choice of, say, just one tulip. Our chosen variety is *Tulipa* 'Queen of Night', but should our taste does not coincide with yours, the Calendar on pages 132-144 offers a **rainbow** of opportunity, since cultivation is the same for all tulips. If *Flower of the Moment* has fired your imagination, specialist reading is the next natural step.

Nigella damascena 'Miss Jekyll' Nigellas are the easiest of hardy annuals; in fact, one packet of seed translates into a lifetime's supply. *Nigella damascena*, said to have been introduced from Damascus over four centuries ago, has fine, feathery leaves that give the plant an ethereal quality. This has inspired its common name – love-in-a-mist. The variety 'Miss Jekyll' has flowers that are bright blue and semi-double.

• The seeds must be sown in finely raked soil because they are too tiny to push through lumps. Mark out drills with a cane, sow the seed, then cover and water. Seedlings will appear in a few days, and these should be thinned out to 15 cm apart as soon as they are big enough to handle.

• Then just stand back and watch the display, remembering to dead-head to prolong flowering. Leave some flower-heads to mature so that the seeds can drop and become next year's seedlings. Autumn-sown seeds make stronger and earlier flowering plants, which are hardy enough to withstand anything the winter throws at them.

Rosa banksiae 'Lutea' Rambling roses are typified by their numerous small flowers held in large bunches, and their habit of sending up long, questing stems from the base. The curved prickles on each stem hook on to any suitable support. Often growing up to 9 m high, they are usually planted to grow through trees or to cover pergolas, where the stems can cascade down.

• Ramblers flower abundantly but briefly, usually in early summer. *Rosa banksiae* 'Lutea', however, breaks the rules. This thornless rambler, with fresh green foliage, carries numerous trusses of yolk-yellow, fully double rosettes that open in late spring. It is the prettiest of ramblers, combining well with wisteria and ceanothus, which flower at the same time, and making a good host for a later-flowering clematis. It is best sited on a warm wall, as it needs protection from frost and likes to be supported on wires.

• Once is has become established, only light pruning is required. After flowering, some of the older side shoots can be cut out, and new growth tied in to replace them. Old and debilitated framework stems can be removed, as long as there is a fresh replacement sprouting from the base. In autumn, vigorous growth made during the summer can be tied in for protection.

• Plenty of manure is the preferred diet for roses, and this should be liberally applied around the base in spring and again in autumn.

Convallaria majalis Lily-of-the-valley has many common names, including Our Lady's tears, fairy bells and May bells. It thrives in moist, cool climates around the world, and is loved by gardeners for its white sprays of waxy bells and delectable perfume.

• Supposedly having a preference for partial shade and soil with plenty of added leaf mould, the rhizomes can be unpredictable and pop up where least expected. Put simply, lily-of-the-valley will grow where it wants to.

• Plant the rhizomes in autumn, placing them 15 cm apart with the tips just below the soil level. They can also be grown in containers, but must be kept in the shade, watered regularly and fed with a liquid fertilizer during the flowering period. Pots can be brought indoors for forcing in early spring so that the fragrance of the flowers can be enjoyed at close quarters.

• Once established, lily-of-the-valley might attempt to overrun an area, so keep it in check by digging up clumps and giving them away or replanting them elsewhere.

• 'Fortin's Giant' is a larger-leaved variety, which has tubbier bells and flowers 10 days later than the common species: a mixture of both will give a succession of flowers.

Dicentra spectabilis 'Alba'

There is no more graceful sight in the May-time garden than the dangling, heart-shaped flowers and divided foliage of the bleeding heart or lyre flower. *Dicentra spectabilis* has rose-pink flowers tipped with white, while the variety 'Alba' has pure white flowers over lighter green leaves.

• Introduced from China during the nineteenth century, dicentras are easy plants to grow, preferring moist but well-drained soil in sun or partial shade. They eventually reach a height and width of 60 cm, and make excellent additions to the late spring border. After flowering, the delicate foliage can become ragged and leave a hole in the summer border, so plunge pots of summer bulbs or annuals into the gap to give continuity of colour.

• The most effective place in the garden for 'Alba' is among shade-tolerant plants that enjoy similar planting conditions: ferns, Japanese anemones and some hardy geraniums complement the form of dicentras, and will take over from them during the summer months.

• Dicentras hate disturbance, and cutting the fragile roots of *D. spectabilis* may well kill it. The best method of propagation is to take root cuttings when the plant is dormant in early spring, and grow them on in sandy compost. You must then wait a year before the cuttings can be planted out.

Erysimum 'Bowles' Mauve' Wallflowers, predominantly in shades of yellow and red, are usually grown as biennial plants, but *Erysimum* 'Bowles' Mauve' has the advantage of being perennial and adaptable enough to thrive in the poorest soil. This superb and vigorous variety quickly forms an upright bush of grey-green leaves up to 90 cm tall and wide. Large, fragrant spikes of single, mauve-purple flowers burst out from their buds in late spring, and will continue to flower throughout the summer if dead-headed regularly.

• The habit and subtle colour of 'Bowles' Mauve' make it a good foil in borders for silver-leaved plants, looking particularly attractive with *Stachys byzantina* or, for a more eclectic companion, the ornamental grass *Helictotrichon sempervirens*. It is also an excellent container plant.

• If 'Bowles' Mauve' has one fault it is that plants have a tendency to become leggy after a couple of years and can flower themselves into an early grave. To avoid this, take cuttings of young leafy shoots in summer; these will root within weeks and can be planted out in spring as replacements.

Wallflowers were often carried at medieval festivals, which has given rise to their botanical name, *cheiranthus,* meaning 'hand-flower'. During Elizabethan times, they were worn to represent a lover's faithfulness in adversity.

• For those who like wallflowers in stronger shades, there are other perennial varieties to choose from. *E. cheiri* 'Bloody Warrior' has a colour that lives up to its name and is heavily perfumed, but needs regular propagation, while *E. c.* 'Harpur Crewe' has sweetly scented, golden-yellow flowers.

Papaver somniferum

Poppies are one of the joys of late spring and early summer, opening their fat buds into papery flowers from the palest of lilacs to rich purple-blacks.

• In Roman mythology *Papaver somniferum* formed part of the garland of Somnus, the god of sleep, who, it is said, created the poppy to free the goddess Ceres from her worries and lull her to sleep. These days the tiny, black seeds of the opium poppy are used widely for culinary purposes, but are also the starting point for your own display of these lovely flowers.

• Seedlings hate to be transplanted, so should be sown directly where they are to flower: either rake out a shallow drill or simply scatter them in finely raked soil. Once they have germinated, which they will in their hundreds, pull some of the seedlings out so that each plant has enough space to grow. In full sun these poppies can reach up to 90 cm in height, but too much competition will result in weedy specimens. Giving them space will also allow the showy, grey-green leaves to be seen to best advantage.

• Once flowering has finished, the plants can be pulled out if the foliage starts to look tatty, but it is worth leaving some in place for the architectural value of the seed heads. These form over the summer, taking on the shape of little pepper pots, and contain thousands of seeds. If allowed to disperse naturally, they will germinate all over the garden, and some of them can be left for earlier flowers next year. If collected, the seeds should be stored in paper bags to keep them fresh for a spring sowing.

‘The garden gets
into full swing
in May ’

Aquilegia vulgaris ‘Nora Barlow’   Although native to open woodland, grassy banks and marshland, aquilegias have been grown in cottage gardens since the thirteenth century. In the wild, they hybridize freely, producing many different variations in colour and flower.

• *Aquilegia* ‘Nora Barlow’ has been in cultivation since the nineteenth century, when it was grown by Miss Barlow, a granddaughter of Charles Darwin. Its pompon-like flowers have numerous spiky petals and an absence of the ‘spurs’ that characterize the common columbine. It is the delicacy of colour that makes ‘Nora Barlow’ unique. The outside tips of the petals are a pale green graduating to a two-tone pale pink and crimson that becomes almost red towards the centre.

• ‘Nora Barlow’ is one of the few varieties of aquilegia that will come true from seed. Leaving it alone and allowing the seed to ripen will result in new plants the following spring, which will bulk up to size and flower the following year. Alternatively, seed can be collected in late summer and sown immediately, then grown on and planted out the following autumn.

• On the whole, aquilegias are very obliging plants, growing in any but the wettest soil and coping with sun or partial shade. They make lovely additions to a woodland planting, producing delicate foliage resembling that of maidenhair ferns. This can be kept fresh by shearing flowered plants to the ground.

• A black-and-white variety called ‘William Guinness’ (also known as ‘Magpie’) is good for more dramatic plantings, while ‘Munstead White’ produces a single, pure white flower and cannot be surpassed for elegance.

Clematis montana 'Elizabeth'   As the word *montana* suggests, this clematis originated in mountainous areas, specifically China and the Himalayas. However, it also describes the plant's habit of growing to almost mountainous proportions, reaching up to 12 m high. *C. montana* is a gardener's ally, growing where almost nothing else will. It will cover dark, cold walls and garden eyesores with attractive foliage, which is smothered in bloom in late spring.

• 'Elizabeth' can be left to rampage over its host, needing very little pruning, and then only to keep it within bounds and out of the guttering if planted against a house wall. Tidy gardeners might feel happier taking the shears to it on a yearly basis, and this should be done immediately after flowering so that new growth can ripen over the summer months to carry next year's flowers.

• The new foliage of 'Elizabeth' opens first to an attractive bronze in the early spring, then matures to a darker green. Its pale pink flowers can take on a whitish hue when planted in dark spots, but the best attribute of this variety is the scent – a warm, vanilla fragrance that can fill a spring day.

• In the wild, clematis seed themselves almost anywhere they are blown by the wind. The most successful are those that find sufficient moisture and some shade from direct sun. Garden-grown clematis need just the same conditions. A thick mulch applied around the root system after planting and then on a regular basis will not only feed the plant, but also keep the roots cool and moist.

Geranium phaeum 'Samobor' Owing to the sombre colour of its flowers, which can vary from deep purple to dark maroon and almost black, *Geranium phaeum* is commonly known as the mourning widow.

• This European native has naturalized itself in areas of the United Kingdom, growing in woods, on banks and by rivers, particularly in eastern Scotland. It is thought to have been introduced towards the end of the sixteenth century. The cultivar 'Samobor' is a fairly recent introduction, which combines the good habits of the species with exceptional foliage – dark green with zonal markings of dark brown. The foliage effect lingers long after the flowers have finished, and looks attractive throughout the summer months.

• Both *G. phaeum* and 'Samobor' are among the few plants that will grow in areas of dry shade, so they may be placed under trees and shrubs, walls and fences, or even in north-facing spots. Adding organic matter to the soil in these areas will, of course, give better conditions for any plant to establish, but one plant of 'Samobor' will quickly bulk up so that divisions can be made for more ground cover.

• The dark colour of the flowers is shown to good effect against shrubs with golden foliage or the white bark of the silver birch, *Betula utilis* var. *jacquemontii*. Hardy geraniums lend themselves well to underplanting schemes of early spring bulbs, such as narcissi and snowdrops, because their growth rapidly disguises the dying foliage of the bulbs.

Geum coccineum There are many varieties of geum to choose from in bright yellows, oranges and reds, but few May flowers can match the jewel-like tones of *Geum coccineum* (sometimes sold as G. 'Borisii'). This quickly forms a dense hummock of bright green, hairy, rounded leaves from which rise hairy, slender stalks bearing the flower-buds on top. When they open, the effect is startling. The bright orange flowers have contrasting centres of prominent, bright yellow stamens and are produced profusely well into June.

• Geums belong to the *Rosaceae* family, and have many cultivars, with new ones being regularly introduced. In nature they grow in meadows, having a preference for moist but well-drained soil. Although they like sun, their easy-going temperament means that partial shade will be tolerated.

• *G. coccineum* is a compact plant, growing to a width and height of just 30 cm, an ideal size for the front of a border.

If there is one criticism, it is that its bright colour may be difficult to place within more pastel schemes. However, it makes an ideal partner for blue plants, such as *Viola cornuta*. Its orange tones can be complemented by euphorbias, the variety 'Fireglow' in particular, and the colour can be softened by the emerging foliage of bronze fennel (*Foeniculum vulgare* 'Purpureum').

• After flowering has finished, the dead heads and stalks should be cut to the base, which may encourage a second crop of flowers to emerge later in the summer. New clumps of geums rapidly become old, and their flowering capacity diminishes. Regular lifting and dividing is necessary in the autumn, perhaps every two years, to keep plants looking and performing at their best.

Paeonia mlokosewitschii There are hundreds of peonies to choose from, but whatever their colour and form, they all herald the coming of summer. The first to be introduced was *Paeonia officinalis* from Crete, widely grown in medieval monastery gardens and highly valued for its foliage as well as its flowers.

- One of the earliest varieties to flower is *P. mlokosewitschii*, commonly known as Molly the witch. It begins to flower in May, making a bowl shape of cool lemon-yellow petals around golden-yellow stamens. As with all peonies, the flowers are fleeting, but this variety is also grown for the beauty of its foliage.
- In late winter or early spring reddish-purple, crinkled foliage begins to emerge, gradually changing to a soft grey-green with a bluish tinge, but retaining some purple markings around the edge. The flowers should not be removed after flowering because the developing seed-heads burst open in autumn to reveal handsome pods of blue-black seeds. Discard any red seeds, as these are not viable, but the black ones, if sown immediately, will germinate the following spring.
- If undisturbed, peonies can live for over 25 years. They thrive in sun and soil that has been well prepared with lots of well-rotted manure. The rhizomatous roots should be planted just below the soil surface: any deeper and they may not flower. Growth should be supported with twiggy sticks early in the season to prevent plants toppling over with the weight of their flowers.
- Once they are planted, it is best not to move peonies, but if this is essential, then September is the best time to do it. Take care not to break off any new buds, which are next year's growth.

Tulipa 'Queen of Night' The tulip is the national flower of Turkey, which is appropriate, as the Turks of the Ottoman Empire were the first to cultivate and hybridize them. In fact, the flower's name is a corruption of *tuliband*, the Turkish word for 'turban', which it resembles in shape.

• 'Queen of Night' is a robust variety, growing to a height of 60 cm. Its satiny petals are the deepest purple, gleaming almost black in the spring sunlight. This glorious tulip enhances all spring planting and looks particularly good in borders with *Allium hollandicum* 'Purple Sensation'.

• Tulips should be planted out as late as November to reduce their chances of succumbing to a potentially fatal disease called tulip fire. Plant them about 15 cm deep in well-drained soil with grit added, and choose a sunny position or the flowers will not open on dull days.

• Once flowering is over and the dead heads have been removed, tulips should be given a general-purpose fertilizer so that the leaves can take in nutrients to build up the bulb for next year's flowering. Gardeners who want to experiment with colour schemes might prefer to discard old bulbs and plant new ones.

During the seventeenth century, tulips were symbols of wealth and power, and the passion for them spread to the Netherlands, where vast sums of money were paid for a single bulb.

JUNE

There is a month when everyone thinks their garden is at its best, and June must surely be top of the list.

June is the ultimate flower-power month. There's such excitement as herbaceous perennials take off and haphazardly scattered annual seeds now spring up in surprising places.

If you are starting from scratch, without a single plant in your garden, and the choices available seem bewildering rather than exciting, this chapter is a shopping list of must-have plants for early summer.

Some very glamorous plants have their moment in June, and while the book title refers to flowering time, it also owes a little to fashion. Even gardeners can become victims of trends, and *Allium christophii* is currently enjoying the spotlight. Its lilac colour couldn't be more 'of the moment', and its outrageous size means it's going to stand out in the crowd.

There are equally glamorous but more discreet contenders for your attention, such as *Alchemilla mollis*, with its zesty lime-coloured heads and sensuous leaves. Get up early to see it dotted with translucent domes of dew, and watch as it seeds itself wantonly in footpaths and borders. This is our idea of a great value-for-money plant, but you may in time have to be strict with it.

We found it extremely difficult to make our choice of geranium because there is a superb choice for virtually every month of the year. Our overall favourite is 'Rozanne', but there are hundreds of garden varieties to choose from. The willing attitude of geraniums means that success is almost always guaranteed, whatever the situation.

But let's not reveal all June has to offer here. Turn the page and let your imagination run riot with the potential of our delectable collection of plants. You will be captivated by the beauty and manageability of each fantastic flower.

Delphinium grandiflorum 'Blue Butterfly'

Once they have reached their flowering potential, delphiniums grow to dizzy heights, and their spires of blooms form the backbone of many herbaceous borders. Each flower is individually beautiful, with the central 'bee' varying in colour from white to black.

• Unfortunately, many small gardens have insufficient space for delphiniums, and many gardeners have insufficient time for the meticulous staking that the classic varieties need to keep them looking perky and upright.

• 'Blue Butterfly' is different. Growing to a height of 45 cm and a spread of 30 cm, its flowers of the most intense electric blue are held along the length of wiry stems rather than in spires. This variety needs no staking, and flowers all summer long. It provides exceptional cut flowers, which need to be cut regularly to increase the length of flowering and prevent the plant from setting seed.

• Delphiniums like to be planted in well-drained soil and sun, overwintered plants forming attractive mounds of foliage that start into growth in early spring. This is the best time to take cuttings from the base or divide them, and also the time to look out for slugs and snails, as the foliage is a major attraction for them. A thick mulch of sharp grit spread at least 30 cm around the emerging plant may act as a deterrent.

• 'Blue Butterfly' is a short-lived perennial, but can be grown as an annual from seed sown in a cold frame in March or April. Seedlings should be ready for planting out in mid-May.

• An easy-to-grow variety of delphinium is the annual larkspur, which gives similar stately blooms and will self-seed around the garden.

Dianthus 'Sops in Wine' Pinks or gillyflowers have been around since Norman monks brought them to Britain in the eleventh century. Since then, hundreds of varieties have been produced, but the 'old-fashioned' pinks, with their compact hummocks of silvery foliage, ragged petals and clove scent, remain enduringly popular. 'Sops in Wine' is one of these. The white flowers are fringed in white with dark centres, and the name relates to when the flowers were steeped in wine to impart their flavour. Every flower is semi-double, scented and produced in quantity.

• Pinks prefer a limy soil – in fact, they top the list of plants that will thrive in chalk – but the main requirement is that the soil should be free-draining.
• The main disadvantage of pinks is that they lose their hummocky habit after a couple of years. Pruning after flowering and feeding will encourage new leaves, but taking cuttings is so easy that replacing plants becomes a better option. Simply choose a strong shoot without flowers on it and cut it off close to the main stem. Remove the lower leaves and trim the cutting to below a leaf joint. Poke the cutting into sandy compost and grow on throughout the summer. It should be planted out into its flowering position in the autumn.

'June is the ultimate flower-power month'

Alchemilla mollis Having leaves shaped like a cloak has given the common name lady's mantle to *Achemilla mollis*. This is a very easy plant to grow, obligingly producing its softly scalloped green leaves and loose sprays of tiny yellow flowers no matter how it is neglected.

• *A. mollis* is a valuable plant for any garden. Although happier in sun, it will grow in light shade, and is excellent for planting along border edges, in gravel or for filling crevices in paving, where it will make a rounded clump about 30 × 30 cm.

• Once you have alchemilla, you will always have it because of its prolific seeding habit. This can be forestalled by going over the plant once it has started to look shabby and pulling away the flower stalks before the seeding process begins. If some seeds do get away, their unwanted seedlings should be weeded out while the plant is young as the rootstock of established plants is tough and difficult to dig out. Alternatively, the entire plant can be cut right back to the ground from late July. The plant will instantly rejuvenate and produce fresh foliage that will linger until November.

Extracting the juice of alchemilla was said to be the first step in changing base metal into gold, and this probably accounts for the plant's Arabic-influenced name: the words *al kimiya* mean 'alchemy'.

■ *Clematis* 'Niobe'   Since its introduction in 1975, *Clematis* 'Niobe' has become a worldwide favourite. The velvety, deep red flowers have contrasting yellow anthers at their centre, and become even darker coloured when the weather is hot. The plant flowers freely over a long period, often lasting until early autumn.

• Although clematis is known for its climbing habit, 'Niobe' is a less rampant variety, reaching only 3 m high.

• Pruning for early, large-flowered cultivars should be carried out in late winter or early spring, when only weak and dead stems should be removed. The remaining stems should be reduced to the highest pair of strong buds, which will bear the early summer flowers.

• In general, clematis is very greedy and will lap up anything that is on offer. To get the best performance, a thick mulch applied around the plant in late winter will give a kick-start in spring. Once new growth appears, give the plant a liquid feed once a week (rose food is ideal) until just before flowering. Resume the liquid feed once the main flush of flowering is over, and this will encourage healthy growth and another crop of flowers.

• Clematis is best planted in the autumn while the soil is still warm so that new roots have a chance to grow before winter sets in. Prepare the soil well, adding lots of organic matter, and place the plant at least 6 cm below the soil level. This allows the clematis to establish a basal crown of buds, which will appear above ground only if the top of the plant becomes damaged or succumbs to wilt.

Geranium 'Rozanne' This hardy geranium is one of the newest introductions and is rapidly proving to be one of the best. From early summer right through to the first frosts it produces prolific quantities of large, iridescent violet-blue flowers with charcoal-grey anthers above mounds of slightly marbled, deep green foliage.

• Like most hardy geraniums, 'Rozanne' will tolerate a planting position in either sun or semi-shade, although full sun will give the best results. Before planting, dig over the soil, add some organic matter and, if the soil is heavy, some grit for drainage. Given this preparation, one plant will rapidly grow to about 60 cm wide and 45 cm tall, making great ground cover for the front of a border, where it will provide a season-long haze of blue and white.

• What makes G. 'Rozanne' remarkable is that it also grows well in patio containers, window boxes and even hanging baskets. When grown in this way, it continuously produces fresh foliage and flowers from its centre. As with any container-grown plant, daily watering and a weekly feed of potassium-rich fertilizer will promote an abundance of cascading flowers.

• Maintenance couldn't be easier: if the plant does start to look a bit unkempt, just clip over it with the garden shears, and fresh foliage and flowers will soon follow. In late autumn, cut the remains of the foliage down to about 15 cm above soil level. In spring, lift and divide if necessary, then place a welcome mulch of organic matter around the crown of the plant.

Astrantia major 'Hadspen Blood'   Since their introduction in the late sixteenth century, astrantias have been stalwarts of the garden, throwing up their unusual flowers from June through to October.

• Astrantias are closely related to cow parsley, fennel, angelica and, surprisingly, carrots: all are members of the umbellifer family. One of the most distinctive features to link all these plants is their flowering heads, which, on close inspection, resemble umbrellas that have been blown inside-out on a windy day.

• Most varieties of *Astrantia major* flower in muted shades of green, white, pink and red, and one of the best and darkest reds is 'Hadspen Blood'. Raised in 1988 by Sandra and Nori Pope, and named after their garden, Hadspen, in Somerset, its charm lies in the multiple flower-heads of dark crimson seemingly held together by even darker bracts positioned delicately on the top of upright stems.

• Although most astrantias thrive in partial shade, it is best to plant 'Hadspen Blood' in well-nourished soil in a sunny position. One plant will expand to cover an area 45 cm wide, while its flowering stems and dark green, palm-shaped leaves rise to a height of 60 cm.

• Astrantias are easy plants to grow, and are rarely troubled by pests or disease. They freely produce fresh flowers and foliage, even after a good chopping back in midsummer. They do best in moist soil, making great border fillers.

• *A. major* 'Shaggy' is another excellent variety to grow, especially in partial shade. When happy, astrantias will produce copious amounts of seed, but self-sown seedlings will often not be as good as the parent, so division in autumn is recommended to increase your stock.

Rosa 'Buff Beauty' To be stalwart, free-flowering and trouble free is a lot to demand from a rose, but 'Buff Beauty' is all these things and more. In flower it is one of the most beautiful hybrid musk roses, opening first in a rich apricot colour, then gradually fading to a creamy yellow.

• The arching branches gradually build up into a compact and graceful bush. Early in the year the stems are covered in young bronze foliage, but the leaves become broad and change to dark green before the flower-buds appear.

• Flowering is continuous throughout the summer, and dead-heading sustains it until the first frosts of autumn. The flowers waft their fruity perfume around the garden and stand up well to any weather the British summer cares to throw at them.

• 'Buff Beauty' is fine in almost any position, as long as it has liberal applications of manure. It will cope with shade, is happy in a container and can even be used to form a hedge, its potential growth being 1.8 × 1.8 m. A well-fed plant will grow to even greater heights, and can be trained against a wall as a climber.

• The vigorous and repeat-flowering hybrid musks need little or no pruning. Any dead, diseased or damaged wood should be removed when the plant is dormant, as should the oldest and least productive stems. Apart from that, they can be left alone. All cuts should be above a healthy bud and slanted in a way that allows any rain or moisture to run away from the bud rather than on to it.

Campanula lactiflora 'Prichard's Variety'

Campanulas have been delightful inclusions to most border schemes since the nineteenth century. The nodding, bell-shaped flowers appear from June onwards.

• The range of varieties is enormous; each has its own habit and charm, but for profuse and long-flowering blooms, 'Prichard's Variety' is in a class of its own. The rich violet-blue flowers are produced in domes atop upright, slender stems clothed with oval leaves. Growing up to 1 m high, this campanula associates well with all shades of roses and makes a good cut flower.

• 'Prichard's Variety' will flower continuously until the autumn, and thrives almost anywhere, tolerating sun and partial shade as long as the soil is moisture-retentive. Compost added at the time of planting ensures quick establishment, and an annual mulch in spring will conserve valuable moisture in the soil.

• Established clumps can be divided in autumn or spring, and cuttings can be taken from the base in early summer. Some staking may be required, and this is best carried out in spring using old twigs, which look more natural. The plant will eventually grow through and conceal the support.

• *C. lactiflora* 'Loddon Anna' is another worthwhile variety, with pale pink flowers, but as it can grow up to 1.5 m tall, it is perhaps better suited to large gardens with deep borders. The stems will need very stout supports to prevent the flowers from toppling over.

🔺 *Viola cornuta* There are very few ground-cover or front-of-border plants that will grow almost anywhere, carpeting the ground with evergreen foliage and flowering non-stop from spring right through to autumn. *Viola cornuta* is one of them.

• When planted in fertile soil (not heavy clay) in sun or partial shade, this plant continuously smothers itself with pale blue flowers. It will rapidly colonize the ground, growing through nearby plants and sometimes hoisting itself upwards into the 'bottom rungs' of nearby shrubs or roses, usefully hiding bare lower stems and creating a tapestry effect to boot. Its pale blue flowers look particularly good next to the acid yellow of *Alchemilla mollis*.

• *Viola cornuta* will flower itself to death, if allowed, so take a pair of shears to it when the plant starts to look straggly, then give it a liquid feed and water well. This will encourage new growth and a second flush of flowers.

The plants also benefit from being divided in the autumn, although cuttings can be taken from non-flowering shoots if any can be found.

• Many varieties of *V. cornuta* are available, including the subtle white 'Alba', the not so subtle greeny-bronze hybrid 'Irish Molly', and the contrasting bronze and purple 'Jackanapes'.

> 'June arrives
> and we know it's going
> to be irresistible'

Digitalis × mertonensis

The wild foxglove, *Digitalis purpurea*, is native to Britain and Europe, and can often be seen growing among ferns or shrubs at the edges of woodland. However, it looks just as glorious towering among plants in the herbaceous border.

• The common foxglove is a biennial, but there are reliable perennial varieties, and *D. × mertonensis* is one of them. It is also called the strawberry foxglove because of its ice-cream-pink flowers, which open from the base of the plant and continue all the way up the stem, making an elegant spire up to 45 cm tall. This is not a fussy plant, as it will grow in either light shade or full sun. After flowering, cut back each stem, and new ones may emerge later in the season.

• The strawberry foxglove breeds true from seed, but gardeners wishing to try this must be patient. During their first year, foxgloves often make nothing more than leaves, building up their resources for a great display in the second year. This plant is more reliably perennial if it is kept on the move, so divide it up after all the flowers are spent, and replant in new positions.

• Other good foxgloves to try are *D. grandiflora*, with creamy yellow flowers (don't disturb this one), and the later-flowering, sun-loving *D. ferruginea*, which has rusty orange flowers.

Eschscholzia californica Scatter eschscholzia's tiny seeds in a dry, sunny part of the garden and you will be rewarded with fine and feathery blue-green foliage followed shortly afterwards by silky, cup-shaped flowers in bright yellow and orange. These California poppies are simple, hardy annuals, which flower right through to late September and bring the 'wow factor' into any garden.

• One packet of seed is the equivalent of a lifetime's supply because the plants are vigorous self-seeders. Sow them in spring for summer flowers, or, in milder areas, in early autumn for a late spring display. Once each poppy has finished flowering, the seed-pods develop, gradually elongating into long, thin curves. Picking the pods is an entertaining pastime, for when they are at their peak of ripeness, they will spring open in your hand, propelling the seeds far and wide.

• California poppies are ideal annuals for the gravel garden, or as edging plants along paths, where they can flop over and soften any hard lines. Once they are established, the only maintenance needed is to thin out the colony from time to time, giving each poppy the space to grow into a sturdy and bushy plant.

During the gold rush of the mid-nineteenth century, the Californian hillsides were covered with dazzling eschscholzias, and naive prospectors thought that the hills really were made of gold.

Lupinus 'Chandelier' Lupins were introduced from North America in 1826, and most of the varieties grown today derive from crosses with the blue *Lupinus polyphyllus*. They are now available in every colour of the spectrum, but the clear lemon-yellow of 'Chandelier' is particularly lovely, lighting up an early summer border.

• Although they will grow in neutral to acid soil, lupins have a preference for slightly acid and well-drained conditions. In the right spot they will produce luxuriant mounds of pale green, starry leaves and candelabras of colour. Remove the spent flower spikes to prolong flowering.

• The foliage of lupins appears very early in the season, so apply a dressing of sharp grit to deter slugs. As an insurance policy against damage, take cuttings from the base of the plant a bit later to make fresh stock. Sturdy plants often have a better chance of survival, so remove any flower spikes in the first year to ensure good root and foliage formation the following year.

• Seed can be collected from the flower spikes and sown the following spring, but the resulting plants will vary considerably from the parents. Many gardeners prefer to sow fresh seed and treat lupins as biennial plants.

Papaver orientale 'Patty's Plum' This is one of the most sought-after oriental poppies on the nursery shelves, having a subtlety of colour unusual in the species. Crumpled silk petals of an almost muddy mulberry deepen towards the middle of the flower, where black blotches surround hair-like stamens. The abundant display of large, sumptuous blooms is brief, but the anticipation of the fat, bristly buds opening to this mouth-watering colour makes up for it.

• In light of its popularity, it is curious to discover that 'Patty's Plum' was condemned by Patricia Marrow, the nurserywoman who raised it, as dull and muddy. She asked Sandra and Nori Pope from Hadspen Gardens to dig it up and take it away, which they did most willingly, and then named it after her.

• Oriental poppies thrive in sun and like soil that is well drained, so if you have heavy soil, add grit before planting. These are very hardy plants, which originated in Armenia, where they grow on rocky slopes and in dry meadows. Their large taproots ensure a tolerance of drought.

• After flowering, the plants tend to become untidy, so cut them right down to the ground and plant over the gap with summer bedding, annuals or summer bulbs. Potted-up seedlings of *Cerinthe major* 'Purpurascens' would fill the gap admirably.

• Propagation of oriental poppies is easy. Simply lift the plants after all the foliage has died down in late autumn and take pieces of root to pot up over the winter.

Iris 'Black Swan' There are thousands of irises available, so it is possible to find a variety that will grow virtually any-where. If there is a criticism to be made of these plants, it is that their flowers are all too fleeting. This makes it doubly important to choose varieties that are exceptional in their flowering so that they pay their way for leaving so soon.

• The colour and texture of *Iris* 'Black Swan' make it highly desirable. The flower stalks rise up from a clump of sword-shaped, upright leaves, and their elongated buds unfurl to reveal a bloom seemingly made of the finest black silk. 'Black Swan' is described as tall, which means that it measures more than 70 cm from the soil to the top of the flower. It is also classified as 'bearded', the beard being the furry line towards the centre of the flower that helps to direct insects to the pollen.

• Bearded irises grow from rhizomes, which store all the energy and food the plant needs to grow and flower. These rhizomes need maximum exposure to sunlight, so they should be planted just above ground level.

• Clumps show their age by producing fewer flowers, so it is a good idea to divide them regularly. Do this either after flowering or in the autumn, discarding old rhizomes in the centre of the clump and any others that have been damaged. Before replanting, cut back the leaves by about half so that the wind does not loosen the young roots.

• 'Kent Pride' is another must-have bearded iris, which has an unusual colouring of rusty brown with buff and apricot markings on the petals.

Allium cristophii Many hundreds of allium species exist, but only a few have become garden plants. One of these is *Allium cristophii*, which can be relied upon to reappear every year. Its large, round heads are borne on strong stems 30 cm tall, and they will often expand to 20 cm wide. Each spherical spray contains up to 75 individual lilac 'stars', each having a metallic sheen and being crisp to the touch.

• The plant's pale green leaves push through the soil from late winter to spring, but wither and die just as the flower-heads are developing. This makes alliums ideal for growing through the developing foliage of later-flowering summer perennials or ground-cover plants, such as hardy geraniums.

• Once flowering is over, the globes gradually turn brown and make seed. The stalks holding these can be cut off at the base and hung upside-down for later use in dried-flower arrangements.

• *A. cristophii* gives a modern, architectural look when grown in containers, and 3–5 bulbs planted 10 cm deep and 3 cm apart will give a great show when placed in a sunny spot. Bulbs are normally available from September onwards, but can be planted until the end of November. Once planted, they are relatively maintenance free, merely requiring a feed with all-purpose fertilizer after they have flowered to build up their strength for the following year.

• Other great varieties to try are *A. hollandicum*, which produces dark purple heads in May, and *A. sphaerocephalon*, which develops small, drumstick-like heads of maroon flowers in July and August.

JULY

Almost every gardening book boasts a cover photographed in July, and this is hardly surprising as it's the month when the quintessential English garden is at its peak. Summer borders are crowded with plants of vertiginous height, either standing elegantly alone or with the natural support provided by their lower neighbours. Above all, the heady scent of old-fashioned sweet peas, lilies and chocolate cosmos gives us a reason to linger in the evening sun because there is only one way a garden can go after its peak… Enjoy it now for as long as possible.

This final push can lead to some daring combinations, and this is one month where any gardener can re-write the rules. If you've got it, flaunt it. Why put your tallest plants at the back of the border if you miss out on their scent? Throw away the colour wheel, for, in our experience, any natural colour combination will work with a backdrop of calming and uniting green.

If you don't like the results, it may just be a matter of re-shuffling. The best time to do this is in the autumn, although on *Gardeners' World* we do show that you can move plants while they are in flower for an immediate effect. This does involve risk when there is so little moisture in the ground and so much heat in the sun, so take extra care of plants you re-site.

If planning a border, visit gardens open to the public. The National Gardens Scheme is a wonderful source of inspiration, while great estates offer big ideas for small gardens. Take a notebook and pencil to write down your favourite combinations: this is an ideal way to become confident and adventurous in your choice of the best July flowers.

Potentilla 'Gibson's Scarlet' There are many varieties of potentilla to choose from, but for sheer razzle-dazzle, 'Gibson's Scarlet' is the one. Its small, open flowers with dark centres are the most brilliant of reds, attracting the attention of bees.

• Potentillas are not for gardeners who like their herbaceous perennials to look tidy. The flowering stems radiate out from a central crown of leaves, spreading along the ground and sprawling through other plants in the border. However, they are not invasive and do not root as they go along: they merely spread to a maximum of 45 cm either side of the plant and simply produce masses of flowers throughout the summer.

• Like their rose, alchemilla and geum relations, potentillas are tough and hardy, they are hardly ever troubled by pests or diseases and will grow in sun and well-drained soil with a bit of moisture at their roots.

• 'Gibson's Scarlet' flowers throughout the summer, continuously throwing out new flowering stems from the central clump, especially if old stems are cut off as soon as the flowers have faded. Impressive clumps develop quickly and, if congested, will affect the quantity of flowering stems. However, potentillas are easy to lift and divide in either spring or autumn.

• Other good varieties include *Potentilla atrosanguinea*, which has glorious silvery foliage and deep maroon flowers, but is not as long-flowering as 'Gibson's Scarlet', and *P. nepalensis* 'Miss Willmott', which has pink flowers and blends well with pastel schemes.

Anthemis tinctoria 'Sauce Hollandaise' This stalwart of any summer border throws out prolific quantities of small daisy flowers on top of wiry stems from early to late summer, reaching its peak of perfection in July. This variety is aptly named because its colour is creamy with a subtle hint of yellow, fading slightly with age.

• *Anthemis tinctoria* 'Sauce Hollandaise' is a plant to be cherished. It will flower so profusely and for such a long time that to approach it with a pair of secateurs may be the last thing on a gardener's mind. But leaving the stems to carry on flowering and become woody will cause exhaustion, and the plant may not recover to flower the following year. Cutting the flowered stems down to the freshest growth at the crown of the plant will ensure that enough light gets in and allow a cushion of new foliage to form. Alternatively, take lots of cuttings from the new growth as an insurance policy for next year.

• The native habitat of *A. tinctoria* is wasteland, so well-drained soil is essential, as is an open, sunny position. Placing it at the front of a border is ideal because here it will grow 1 m high and wide; if placed near a path, the flowers can flop over to soften any hard edges. Other good varieties include 'Wargrave Variety' and 'E.C. Buxton', which are pale yellow. A May-flowering variety is *A. punctata* subsp. *cupaniana*, which has startling white flowers over silver filigree foliage.

Anthemis makes good cut flowers and is an essential ingredient in summer posies, so plant it in places where it is readily accessible.

> 'July is often the month when the garden is at its peak'

■ *Knautia macedonica* With its elegant but low-growing, grey-green leaves, *Knautia macedonica* is a choice perennial for any garden, ideal at the front of the border. As a member of the scabious family, it has flowers resembling pincushions on stalks, but in this variety the stalks are profuse, each one topped with dark crimson, double, globular buttons about 2 cm across. The stalks rise to a height of 60 cm, which means that they rarely dominate a bed and never hide what is planted behind.

• *K. macedonica* likes a sunny spot in the garden, preferably in well-drained soil, where it will seed and move around once happy in its situation. In the spring, so-called Irishman's cuttings can be taken; these have a piece of root attached and can be planted out directly into the soil, but they must be nurtured and watered regularly.

• This plant always seems to look best growing alongside ornamental grasses of a similar height: *Stipa arundinacea* has a bronze softness to its leaves, which contrast well with the crimson buttons of the knautia and allow them to poke through, while *Helictotrichon sempervirens* has silver leaves that provide a good contrast to knautia, as well as making an excellent background when planted behind it.

• What makes this plant a worthwhile addition to all gardens, especially small ones, is its extraordinarily long flowering habit. Established plants will start as early as May, reaching their peak in July, when the flowers will be alive with bees, and continuing to produce flowering stems until as late as December. Dead-heading encourages more flowers, but is not essential, as the spent flower-heads turn pale green and retain their button-like shape.

summer : july

Penstemon 'Blackbird' The graceful, airy and companionable *Penstemon* 'Blackbird' grows 90–120 cm high and has virtually ever-green leaves. The dusky purple flowers appear scantily from late May, reaching a crescendo in high summer, and can sometimes continue through to November in a sheltered spot – a blessing for a small garden.

• The phenomenal flowering power is encouraged by continuous dead-heading throughout the summer, snipping at a point where new shoots are emerging below the spent flower stem. A general-purpose fertilizer in spring and a foliar liquid feed (tomato fertilizer) aid the continuing display.

• The purple shade of 'Blackbird' both blends and contrasts well with other colours, such as red, pink and yellow, and even cools the fiery oranges of late-flowering perennials. It looks particularly good with the ornamental grass *Stipa arundinacea*.

• All penstemons hate having cold, wet feet in winter. To thrive they need well-drained, fertile soil, full sun and ample water during dry periods. Add plenty of compost and horticultural grit to the soil before planting. Do not prune in autumn, as the summer growth will protect the crown of the plant over the winter. Instead, wait until the weather is kinder in March or April, then cut back to about 15 cm above any new growth from the soil.

• A hard winter or old age will defeat penstemons, so cuttings taken in late summer or early autumn will ensure stock for the following year. Non-flowering side shoots planted in gritty compost, 3–5 cuttings to a pot, will soon root and can be potted up individually. Some winter protection, such as a cold frame, will almost always ensure a respectable-sized plant in full flower the following summer.

Lathyrus odoratus 'Painted Lady' Sweet peas have been grown in Britain since 1699, when they were introduced from Sicily. 'Painted Lady' appeared about forty years after the original plants were introduced, and by the end of the century seeds were available for sale.

• This sweet pea produces two flowers per stem, which are smaller than those of the more cultivated varieties, but their intensity of fragrance will fill a garden. The top petal or 'banner' of the bicoloured flowers is dark pink, while the side and lower petals are white. 'Painted Lady' has a bushy habit and will climb to a height of 1.2–1.5 m given plenty of sun and lots of water.

• Sweet peas climb by putting out delicate tendrils that coil around the support of canes, wires or other plants. By far the best way to show them off is to grow them up a willow wigwam: this not only gives the tendrils plenty of fine twigs to grasp, but also allows easy access for picking.

• 'Painted Lady' is the definitive cut flower to bring into the house as blooms must be cut every day to ensure continuous flowering until autumn. The plant will rapidly go downhill and stop producing flowers if seed is allowed to form.

• Another fantastically scented sweet pea is *L. odoratus* 'Matucana', which has deep purple and dark red flowers. For a more subtle colour, choose the creamy white 'Mrs Collier'.

Geranium 'Ann Folkard' An outstanding hardy geranium
for a sunny position is 'Ann Folkard'. While its golden foliage and
magenta flowers don't, at first, seem a very tasteful combination,
they look extremely good in a border.

• In spring a mass of yellow-green
foliage emerges, which quests in all
directions, through and over other plants.
As midsummer approaches, saucer-
shaped, silky magenta flowers appear
along the long stems, each flower having
a fine tracery of black veins that leads
down to a black 'eye' in the centre.
• This exceptional display continues
throughout the summer until the first
frosts, with the central crown continually

producing fresh foliage and new crops
of flowers. Old flowering stems can be
cut back to the central crown throughout the summer to keep the foliage
looking fresh.
• 'Ann Folkard' is never invasive, will
not root along its stem to become a
nuisance and, being sterile, will not set
seed. It can be propagated by dividing
the plant in spring, just as new growth
is emerging.

Galtonia candicans One
of the most elegant of summer-
flowering bulbs, *Galtonia
candicans* can be plunged or
planted among earlier-flowering
perennials. Its 1 m-tall spires
of fragrant, waxy, white hanging
bells look like huge hyacinths,
and will give added value to
the same patch of ground.

• This plant is excellent for sunny sites,
as long as the soil is moist, well drained
and well fed. These conditions are sometimes hard to guarantee in the garden,
so it is often better to plant the large
bulbs in pots, where watering conditions
can be more controlled. The whole pot
can then be plunged into the garden at
flowering time for removal later. As the
foliage is rather floppy and looks tatty
after flowering, the plunging option is a
good one; otherwise, galtonias can be
planted behind penstemons or among
agapanthus, both of which disguise the
foliage of the galtonias.

• Spires of finished flowers will make
lots of seed that may well self-sow.
Collected seed sown in the spring will
eventually make a flowering-sized bulb
after 2–3 years. Offsets can be gleaned
from the bulbs in either the autumn or
spring, and replanted to bulk up rather
sooner.

• *G. princeps* is an earlier-flowering species
than *candicans*, and is also shorter and
stockier. Like the later-flowering and
more tender *G. viridiflora*, it has racemes
of unusual pale green flower bells, which
make good cut flowers.

Clematis 'Etoile Violette' The choice of clematis is over-whelming; we could easily have chosen one for every day, let alone one a month, but we narrowed our choice for July to problem-free species and their cultivars. These may have slightly smaller flowers, but they are not attacked by clematis wilt. Native to southern Europe and Turkey, *Clematis viticella* and hybrids such as this are hardy, robust, disease-free and easy to maintain.

• 'Etoile Violette' rampages into growth early in the year, reaching a height of 3 m within weeks. All the questing stems are usually smothered in buds that burst open to reveal dark purple flowers with bright golden centres. The display will reach a crescendo in July, but go on intermittently until the early autumn, so the plant will appreciate feeding (see page 53).
• Pruning this clematis couldn't be easier. Wait until early February, when it is already showing signs of growth, and cut it down to just above a pair of buds about 30–45 cm above soil level. If growing through evergreen trees or shrubs, and the messy growth will spoil the look of the host over the winter months, this clematis can be cut back by about two-thirds in late autumn.
• Other good *viticella* clematis are the deep red 'Kermesina' and the sixteenth-century variety *C. v.* 'Purpurea Plena Elegans', which has double, smoky mauve flowers.

Lilium regale The trumpet-shaped blooms of *Lilium regale* are striking in several ways. The wine-stained petals on the outside open to white inside, revealing golden filigree anthers, and the fragrance, especially in the early morning and late evening, is memorably powerful. One or more flowers are carried on top of stems 1–1.8 m tall, which are clothed in narrow, purple-green leaves.

• The secret of growing lilies successfully is to plant the bulbs deeply in rich, well-drained soil in early autumn. Enrich the soil with compost or manure, make planting holes 10–15 cm deep, add a 2.5 cm layer of grit and place a bulb in each hole. Regal lilies start into growth in early spring, so may need some protection from late frosts.

• Growing lilies in pots allows them to be treated as a sort of 'moveable feast'. When in full flower, use the pots to fill gaps in the border, and lift them out again once flowering is over. Shorter varieties can be grown as patio pot plants: try 'Stargazer', which has deep pink flowers with speckled markings, or 'Casa Blanca', which is a good white.

The fragrance of *Lilium regale* has a potency that is almost intoxicating. This is attributed to it containing a chemical called indol, which is widely used by perfumers. Unusually, however, the scent of the lily cannot be extracted from the flower as essential oil.

Verbascum chaixii 'Album'

Many varieties of verbascum can be short-lived, needing to be regularly propagated by root cuttings. *Verbascum chaixii* 'Album' is different – it's easy to grow and reliably perennial. This verbascum enjoys a gritty soil and lots of sun, but does not seem to mind quite heavy soil. It will successfully flower in the shade of other plants, which is where it looks best, giving a vertical accent to border planting.

• This plant is very easy to grow from a packet of seeds planted in early spring, just as the weather becomes milder. A warm windowsill or greenhouse will start them off into growth, but they must be regularly potted on until they have developed a good root system before planting out. Retaining the last flower spikes of the season (and resisting the temptation to tidy the plant up by cutting them off) often results in new seedlings appearing the following year. Self-sown seedlings sometimes flower in their first year, albeit a bit later in the season.

• Other good verbascums to try are *V.* 'Gainsborough', with pale yellow flowers, and 'Cotswold Queen', with dark-eyed apricot flowers. Some of the new introductions, such as 'Helen Johnson' and 'Megan's Mauve', walk off the nursery shelves in summer. They are gorgeous, but root cuttings need to be taken from them yearly as they are not reliably perennial. If you can't live without them, why not treat them as bedding and buy new ones every year?

Cosmos atrosanguineus This graceful flower, whose name means 'beautiful dark blood-red', has dark-centred, maroon-crimson blooms of a velvety texture, which hover over the plant on slender stems 45 cm high. The foliage is dark green, sometimes with a purplish tinge to the edges, and spreads to cover an area of 60 cm. The common name is 'Chocolate Cosmos' because its fragrance is like stepping into a chocolate shop.

• Chocolate cosmos is not fully hardy. It needs sun and moisture, and can be difficult to overwinter. It grows from tubers and, theoretically, can be lifted and stored in the same way as dahlias. However, it is less plump and does not always survive this treatment. A generous mulch will protect the crown and roots, while a cloche (plastic is fine) will keep it warm. The cloche also serves as a reminder of where the plant is, as new shoots will not form on it until late spring when many gardeners will have thought the plant lost anyway.

• Its limited spread, height and tender habit make *Cosmos atrosanguineus* ideal for growing in containers on a sunny patio, where it can be watered daily, regularly dead-headed and given a weekly liquid feed. When flowering is over, the pot and plant can be enveloped in bubble-wrap or stored in a frost-free place.

The final push can lead to some daring combinations

■ *Alcea rosea* 'Nigra' The hollyhock is the quintessential cottage garden plant, its lofty flowers reaching 2 m or more in the space of a few months. Being a short-lived perennial, it is more often grown as a biennial.

• Hollyhocks are available in almost every colour, except blue. The variety 'Nigra' produces its frilly, single petticoats in a silky, dark purple that fades with age to black. The yellow variety 'Chater's Double' covers its stout stems with blooms that resemble huge-skirted ballgowns.

• Unfortunately, hollyhocks are prone to rust disease, and the only way to treat this is to spray with a protective fungicide before May, when the trouble appears, and repeat the treatment later.

• Raising fresh plants from seed will ensure a rust-free start in life, and seed should be sown in spring for flowers the following year. Pot them on, giving them the shelter of a cold frame and planting them out the following spring.

• Hollyhocks like heavy, rich soil in full sun or light shade, but will tolerate other soils, often self-seeding in cracks in paving. A mulch of compost or manure in the autumn will replace the nutrients used up by the plant in making its huge growth.

• Lots of moisture is essential in dry weather, and the tall stems need staking to protect them from wind damage. More compact and robust plants with plentiful flowers can be made by pinching out the main stem, which encourages side shoots; these, in turn, can be pinched out. Eventually a sturdy and bushy plant will form that will not be as tall but requires no staking.

Eryngium giganteum The weird beauty of eryngiums or sea hollies is one of the surprises of the horticultural world. Few people would guess that these plants belong to the same family as astrantias, cow parsley and fennel.

• Eryngiums are mostly perennial, but *E. giganteum*, or Miss Willmott's ghost, is a biennial. The common name derives both from Ellen Willmott's surreptitious habit of distributing seeds in friends' gardens, and the plant's silvery-grey bracts, which do have a ghostly quality when they appear. The flower-heads are covered by millions of tiny hairs, which stop the wind and sun from reaching the stomata (pores) on the leaf surface and drying it out.

• Eryngiums need sunny, free-draining conditions to thrive, so they are well suited to patches of stony soil or gravel gardens, where they reach an eventual height and spread of about 90 cm.
• Unlike other perennial forms of eryngium, Miss Willmott's ghost is monocarpic, which means that it dies once it has flowered. However, it will seed itself about, and the resulting seedlings will flower in their second year if there is not too much competition from

other plants. Surprises are one of the joys of gardening, and it is always exciting to find new plants in unexpected places.
• Silvery eryngiums are good companions to many other plants, adding to the cool nature of a soft pastel border, or providing contrast to 'hot' planting combinations. Good perennial varieties that create a similar effect are the metallic blue *E. × oliverianum*, which grows to 60 cm, and *E. bourgatii*, which reaches the same height but has smaller flowering heads.

Hemerocallis citrina The common name for hemerocallis is daylily because the flowers last for only one day. As there are many dazzling varieties to choose from, selection can be difficult, and it is easy to overlook the simplicity and beauty of species such as the scented *Hemerocallis citrina*.

• This is a daylily with a difference because it opens at night. The narrow flowers are many and large (9–12 cm long on stems up to 75 cm high) and their lemon-yellow colour shows up especially well in the night garden.

• The leaves of *H. citrina* form a compact clump, but are coarser than those found on most daylilies: broad, dark green and with a glaucous underside, they can, like most hemerocallis foliage, look tired once flowering has finished. If they are cut down to the ground, another crop of fresh leaves will emerge, but the following year's flowering may not be so abundant. Hemerocallis thrive in sun or partial shade, tolerate any soil as long as it is not too dry and can be planted at almost any time of year. They also respond well to being divided every three years, or when the flowering performance is not so good.

• For flowering from summer to the first frost and compactness of habit choose *H*. 'Stella de Oro', which has orange-yellow flowers. *H*. 'Corky' is an earlier-flowering, scented variety, while the fiery red and yellow mix of *H*. 'Stafford' will flower from mid- to late summer.

Diascia rigescens The low habit of *Diascia rigescens* makes it an ideal plant for the front of a border or raised bed, where the flowering stems can sprawl over the edge. This trailing perennial plant makes a dense mat of heart-shaped leaves and has 30-cm spires of salmon-pink flowers from summer right through to early autumn.

• It grows naturally in the damp forest margins and grasslands of South Africa, so in a garden situation it likes moist soil enriched with compost and some grit added for good drainage.

• Because of its flowering habit, *D. rigescens* makes a good container plant, and is also suitable for hanging baskets: the flowering stems will be upright in the middle but grow downwards and out from the sides.

• Maintaining the plant's summer display is easy: simply clip over it with a pair of shears when it starts to look straggly. As with most prolific flowerers, this seems cruel, but shearing off all the spent flowers will rejuvenate it.

• Although this plant is not reliably hardy, it will survive a not-too-hard winter. However, to ensure plants for next year, take cuttings in the autumn and give them some protection while they overwinter.

• Many varieties of diascia are sold as bedding plants in the summer. Of these, 'Blackthorn Apricot' and *D. barberae* 'Salmon Supreme' make lovely contributions to the front of a border, and can also be grown in containers.

AUGUST

This can be a tricky month for all but the most dedicated of gardeners, since the vast majority of us go on holiday and leave our gardens to whatever the weather throws at them. Returning from a two-week absence to find that your particular favourites have flowered while you were away can be pretty annoying, so here we have provided a succession of irresistible plants.

Despite the unpredictable nature of our weather, we now enjoy a warmer climate, which allows us to indulge our ever-increasing taste for the exotic and to experiment with tropical and sub-tropical themes. Our selections reflect this mood: agapanthus and eucomis are native to South Africa, *Angelica gigas* originates in the Far East, and *Verbena bonariensis* comes from South America. Verbena flowers earlier than August and continues until November, so it's easy to understand why it is seen in all the best gardens.

Many of our other choices were imported by adventurous plant-hunters between the seventeenth and nineteenth centuries. They are now so familiar in British gardens that it is difficult to imagine them in a more natural setting. While they all take varying degrees of care, they are surprisingly tolerant of our absences during the height of summer.

If you are going away, it's second nature to arrange care for pets and houseplants, but don't forget the garden. Friends and family will gladly water your borders and pots if you offer to return the favour. Moving pots to shadier parts of the garden and using water-retaining gels will help keep your plants nourished while you are away. Lawns can be left to their own devices – they will always recover.

Agapanthus

For a touch of blue to cool
down the harsh light of late
summer, agapanthus is a
glorious perennial to choose.
The lily of the Nile, as it is also
known, is a fleshy-rooted
perennial, not from Egypt as
the name suggests,
but a native of South Africa.

• Some agapanthus species are tender,
but many hybrids are hardy to at least
-15 °C. These compact plants reach a
height of 45 cm and have shiny, strappy
leaves from which the stems emerge
bearing buds that can seem slow
to open.
• They eventually form a sphere of
many small, lily-shaped blue blooms
that last for about four weeks before
forming seed.
• To perform at their best agapanthus
need lots of sun, moisture and regular
feeding with tomato fertilizer. They
thrive on congestion, so are perfect
for containers, where they can stay
for years with just a top-dressing of fresh
compost and some all-purpose fertilizer
in spring.
• Once the show of flowers gets a bit
scarce, wait until spring before dividing
up the clumps and replanting them in
fresh compost. Patience may be required,
however, as flowering may not happen
in the first year after division.
• Good varieties of agapanthus include
'Loch Hope' (left), one of the tallest at
1.5 m, Headbourne hybrids, and 'Midnight
Star', which is an outstanding dark blue.
For other shades, it is often best to wait
until nurseries have the plants in flower
before making a selection.

Phlox paniculata Varieties of *Phlox paniculata* come in many shades, ranging from white through pink to mauve and magenta. They are an asset to the late summer garden, filling the air with a warm, summery scent. They are greedy plants, needing lots of manure when planted, water during the growing season and a top-dressing of compost or manure in the spring. If some of the growing tips of the new shoots are pinched out when they are about 30 cm high, the plants will grow bushier and enjoy prolonged flowering.

• A common problem of phlox is powdery mildew, often indicative of dryness at the roots. To avoid this, plant them in partial shade where the soil is moister. Another problem is eel-worm, which causes twisted, wispy leaves and thin stems. The only answer is to lift and burn the affected plants and avoid growing phlox in the same spot for at least three years.

• Propagation can be done by taking cuttings from new shoots in the spring, or by dividing the roots. (Root cuttings will be unaffected by eel-worm and will make cleaner plants.)

Romneya coulteri The Californian tree poppy is the queen of all poppies, the dazzling white and silky petals surrounding a central mass of golden stamens. The flowers, up to 15 cm across, have a sweet fragrance, and the foliage is just as dramatic – glaucous and silver grey with a deeply jagged outline. Established clumps of romneya can cover a big space in the garden – perhaps 2 m high and wide.

• Romneya is classed as a sub-shrub, which is halfway between a shrub and herbaceous perennial. In its native habitat in the Santa Ana Mountains of southern California it grows on dry river-beds and in canyons. The best position for this choice plant is therefore one that will give plenty of sun and a well-drained, even stony soil – perhaps in a gravel garden or by a warm wall.

• Although romneyas can take ages to establish, once settled they will make large colonies, their roots popping up well away from the original plant. These roots are sensitive to damage, and although suckers may be dug up for potting or replanting, they will, in the main, refuse to root.

• Root cuttings taken during the winter should be planted vertically and individually in small, biodegradable pots and placed in a heated propagator.

Once the roots have filled the pot, they can be potted on until they become well-established plants and can be planted outside. The price of well-established, pot-grown plants in nurseries reflects the difficulty of propagation.

• Romneyas are perfectly hardy and will respond if cut to the ground in early winter. This ruthless treatment ensures that the plant remains at a manageable height the following year.

Verbena bonariensis It is surprising that one of the most popular plants of the past decade was first introduced from South America as early as 1726. Whether grown as a single specimen or in large groups, *Verbena bonariensis* is eye-catching. It is an airy plant, waving its dense clusters of tiny, pale purple flowers at the top of tall, square stems that can be as high as 1.5 m. Planted through a border, it makes any mixed planting coherent, the lofty flowers giving the impression of dozens of ultraviolet lights hovering in the air.

• What makes this verbena exceptional is that it takes up a mere 15 cm of growing space. The flower stems are branching and sturdy and never need support, so despite being head-high, this verbena can be planted at the front of a border where any planting beyond is never obscured.

• In its native habitat, *V. bonariensis* grows in marshy ground, so summer moisture is essential to its tall flowering habit. However, it is not reliably hardy, so planting it in well-drained soil with some added grit will increase the chances of survival. Winter survivors will start to flower earlier in the year than younger plants, which make their appearance later in the summer, flowering prolifically into autumn and carrying on spasmodically until November.

• One of the fun elements of *V. bonariensis* is that it will seed everywhere. Come the spring, the seedlings pop up in unexpected places, deciding for themselves where they want to grow.

> 'August provides a succession of irresistible plants'

Helenium 'Moerheim Beauty'   Heleniums are late summer bloomers, with daisy-like flowers in bright shades of yellow and orange. 'Moerheim Beauty' has dark, orange-red flowers tinged very slightly with yellow on the outside. The petals of this variety radiate and reflex backwards, as if offering the dark brown centres to the sun.

- This is an easy plant to grow in almost any soil, as long as it is not too wet and gets full sun. With plenty of moisture and limited competition, heleniums will quickly form a good clump of narrow, dark green leaves, eventually covering an area of 60 cm. These clumps will need frequent division in spring to keep the plant young and flowering well.
- The flowering stems of 'Moerheim Beauty' will rise to a height of 90 cm, starting to flower in late July, reaching a peak in August and, if dead-headed

regularly, continuing until September. This display is most effective if the clumps are planted in threes as part of a 'hot' colour scheme. Alternatively, they provide a good contrast to the bronze foliage of phormiums or the feathery foliage of bronze fennel.
- *H.* 'Wyndley' has orangy-yellow flowers and the same compact habit as the rich yellow 'Butterpat'. The bright yellow 'Sonnenwunder' will grow to 1.5 m, as will the yellow-and-maroon 'Riverton Gem'.

The helenium, so the legend goes, got its name as the flower that sprang up from the tears of Helen of Troy. Less romantically, the common name is sneezeweed.

Cerinthe major 'Purpurascens'   Cerinthe looks its best at the height of summer. After it has been baked by the sun, the plant's leaves turn from grey to a glaucous, luminous blue. The foliage effect is so stunning that it really need not bother to flower, but it does, producing purply-blue bracts from which tube-like, dark purple flowers appear. It is around these flowers that bees buzz continuously, and in which the little black seeds can be clearly seen once each flower has finished.

• Although cerinthe is an annual plant in most gardens, it can be perennial in warmer, sheltered places. It drops loads of seed towards the end of the summer, which rapidly germinate where they fall. The subsequent seedlings do not survive the wet and cold of winter unless protected, so it is best to collect as many seeds as possible and save them for sowing in late spring the following year.

• Cerinthe is a stunning border plant, making a dense mound 45 cm across and 30 cm high. It looks fantastic with blue-leaved plants, such as eryngiums, or growing at the base of the tall, silver-leafed perovskia. It also grows very successfully in containers.

Ipomoea tricolor 'Heavenly Blue' Ipomoea is also known as the morning glory, and 'Heavenly Blue' is a beautiful example of it. The saucer-shaped flowers open to the morning sun, making it ideal for 'dressing-gown gardeners', who take their first cup of tea while walking round the garden to find out what's happened overnight.

• Known for its climbing habit, ipomoea always twines clockwise around its support, and is best grown up an obelisk or wigwam of canes. If grown through another plant, or planted against too chunky a support, it can become over-tangled and lose its sense of direction.

• Ipomoea is an easy-to-grow annual, which can be started off in a greenhouse in early spring, or sown outside in late spring. (The seeds will not germinate unless the soil temperature is above 10 °C.) The seeds have a hard coating, so they benefit from being soaked overnight before sowing. They are best sown three seeds to a pot, then the whole pot can be planted out once the seedlings have reached 30 cm in height. At this size they will be more than ready to start twining upwards.

• Make sure that the site chosen gets the morning sun and a fresh crop of flowers will appear every day, continuing as late as October. Once the buds reach the 'rolled-up umbrella' stage, set the alarm clock for an earlier than usual start so you can enjoy the morning show at its best.

Nicotiana sylvestris Evening fragrance for the August garden is provided by one of the giants of the tobacco family, *Nicotiana sylvestris*. A late April sowing of the fine seed on either a windowsill or in a warm greenhouse can be planted out in May, and 12 weeks later will have formed into rosettes of huge, weed-smothering, sticky leaves and stems up to 1.5 m tall.

• *N. sylvestris* adds great presence and a voluptuous aroma to the night garden. The long, tubular white flowers droop down *en masse* from the top of long, sturdy stems, keeping firmly closed in strong sunshine, but opening all together at the first hint of sundown. They are a magnetic attraction to night-feeding moths that love to drink the nectar.

• The tobacco plant is tolerant of sun, but prefers partial shade, the back of a border being ideal. A group of three planted in a front garden will not only make an architectural statement, but the scent will waft into every open window on a warm evening, and greet passers-by and visitors with nosefuls of perfume.

• Nicotianas enjoy rich soil, so organic matter dug in before planting will guarantee huge leaves and tall stems. Flowering goes on for many weeks, and copious amounts of very fine seed are produced at the end of the season. This seed is scattered far and wide and will often germinate immediately. In sheltered town gardens, seedlings may well over-winter, and the main plant too, but rather than risk loss, seed collection is recommended for sowing the following spring.

Angelica gigas Few plants can match the drama and architecture of the biennial herb *Angelica gigas*. From the bold, shiny and large green leaves thick purple stems rise to a height of almost 1.8 m, holding pouch-like leaf sheaths at the top. The sheaths are gradually forced open and umbels of beetroot-coloured flowers emerge.

• *A. gigas*, a recent introduction from the Far East, is striking in form and flower, ideal for punctuating later-flowering perennials, such as ornamental grasses. This angelica likes sun and rich, moist soil. While it does produce seed, it tends to deteriorate after 2–3 months, so seed should be collected and sown as soon as it is ripe in September. *A. gigas* behaves like a true biennial, dying away in its second year.

• The more common *A. archangelica* is equally dramatic, producing huge green leaves and round heads of greenish-white flowers in late spring. The flowers remain on the plant throughout the summer before drying to a parchment brown. This angelica does best in deep, moist soil in partial shade, and can be maintained as a perennial, albeit short-lived, if the flowering stem is cut down and prevented from setting seed. This treatment will keep the plant going for about four years.

Monarda 'Cambridge Scarlet' The rich red display of hooded flowers on 'Cambridge Scarlet' is arranged on top of 1 m-high stems over hairy, aromatic leaves. This variety is best placed where the leaves can be fondled because this releases their fragrance into the air.

• Monardas tend to suffer from mildew during the summer if their roots get too dry. This can be avoided by planting them in partial shade, where moisture loss is not so problematic. Alternatively, lots of bulky organic matter added to the soil in sunnier planting sites will prevent it drying out, as will regular watering.

• In winter the whole plant dies down quickly, but then small rosettes of dark green leaves appear, which can kill themselves off by overcrowding. Division in spring is advisable, but as the flowering of monardas tends to decline after three or four years, they are best taken out and replaced by new plants.

• The pink variety 'Croftway Pink' or the purple 'Prärienacht' (Prairie Night) are softer shades that would work well in muted planting schemes.

Kniphofia 'Little Maid'

Red-hot pokers or torch lilies add drama to planting, throwing up spires of colour from knee height to head high in varying flame shades over coarse, strappy leaves. Kniphofias have been out of favour in domestic gardens for some time, but are now becoming the latest in 'designer' planting.

• If their hot shades and space-grabbing habit do not find favour with small garden owners and more pastel schemes, then *Kniphofia* 'Little Maid' will. Raised in 1966 by Beth Chatto, 'Little Maid' is dainty and sophisticated, reaching a height of only 60 cm. The leaves are grass-like and arching, forming a small clump from which slender stems rise. The flower-buds that form from these open up in a creamy white colour and age to pale lemon.

• Kniphofias are native to South Africa, growing in wet, marshy soil, so they like similar conditions in a garden and lots of sun. Although hardy, these plants may die from cold, wet feet in winter, so adding grit to the soil when planting will give them a better chance of survival. They require lots of moisture as soon as new growth starts in the spring.

• 'Little Maid' looks particularly good if grouped in gravel plantings; the gravel acts as a mulch, preventing excessive moisture loss during the summer and providing protection and drainage in the winter. Dividing established clumps in the spring will ensure good flowering.

• A tender, elegant species is the coral red *K. thomsonii*, again ideal for gravel plantings. More flamboyant varieties include the earlier-flowering 'Bees' Sunset' in shades of flame, and the taller classic red-and-orange 'Alcazar'.

Eucomis bicolor Green flowers are unusual additions to any garden, but the architectural green spikes of eucomis make a bold statement in late summer. The maroon-flecked, upright stems bear a column of star-shaped green flowers with dark-red margins. The leafy tuft that springs out from the top of the flower gives the plant its common name, pineapple flower.

• *Eucomis bicolor* enjoys sun and well-drained soil, so an addition of grit at planting time is advisable. One bulb will rapidly form a colony of plants 30–45 cm high and wide. The flowers look good at the front of a border with red or orange dahlias growing behind them.

• Eucomis are large, South African bulbs of borderline hardiness, but winter protection is easy. Those grown in the ground can be mulched to protect the crown and covered with a plastic cloche, while those grown in pots can be brought into a frost-free place and stored dry until the following spring.

• The flower spike lasts the whole of the summer and into autumn before dying back to a central crown. Once the flowering performance has diminished, clumps will need to be divided. This can be done in the spring while they are still dormant. Dig up clumps and separate the offsets, or tip the plants out of their pots, divide and replant them, and bring them into life with a little watering.

SEPTEMBER

In September the garden slows down, the **fading** heads of summer flowers just ghostly reminders of the riotous colours that preceded them. Our selections for this month match that **mellow** mood, and we add to the sense of nostalgia by including some plants that are enjoying a return to popularity.

The days when dahlias were relegated to the allotment for cut flowers or grown for exhibition are long gone. Fashion always turns full circle, and dahlias are currently the essence of the bold and **flamboyant** colour schemes, just as they were in Victorian times.

The opportunities to increase your flowers of the moment at this time of year are immense; in fact, this can be the most productive time to garden. An **energetic** weekend of bulb planting, for example, can provide you with flowers in as little as four months. Snowdrops, crocuses, daffodils and alliums will fill the garden from January to June.

This is also a great way to encourage the next generation of gardeners, since planting bulbs is child's play. All it needs is some well-drained soil, a few bulbs and a little patience.

In September the soil is still warm, so it's the **perfect** time to get plants in the ground. Except for frost-tender plants, which should be brought indoors, plants will benefit from an autumn planting and will grow much **stronger**.

Don't forget to take stock of what's already in the garden. Plants that flowered earlier in the year may have continued to make **architectural statements** with their seed-heads, and in a final generous gesture, many of these will now burst to supply a new generation of plants. Their **seed** can be collected and stored over the winter months, then sown in the spring. If ever a month symbolized the cycle of life, it must surely be September.

Helianthus 'Velvet Queen' Although there are some lovely perennial varieties of helianthus, most of them grow to fairly monstrous proportions, so are best suited to large gardens with deep borders. There is much more fun and variety to be had from *Helianthus annuus*, the annual sunflower, which is produced in new varieties and new colours every year.

• 'Velvet Queen' has been around for some time and is a firm favourite with many gardeners. The flowers have a velvety texture and are a glorious, deep red with a chocolate-brown centre, but the exact shade varies with each bloom. Although it has the typical dark green foliage of all sunflowers, 'Velvet Queen' grows to a 'mere' 1.5 m. Like all sunflowers, it acts as a magnet to bees and, once seed is formed, birds of every kind will visit to feed.

• Seeds can be sown about 1cm deep directly into the soil or in pots. They germinate rapidly in late spring, and once the soil is warm enough, they will rocket out of the ground, quickly filling the back of borders. Seedlings will need protection from slugs at first, but require no other special attention apart from regular watering.

• 'Velvet Queen' looks fantastic with the annual red-leaved orach *Atriplex hortensis* var. *rubra*, and makes good cut flowers. To form a bushier plant with more flowers for either cutting or display, pinch out the growing point once the plant has reached about 90 cm in height.

Crocosmia × crocosmiiflora 'Emily McKenzie'   Over a century of breeding has produced hundreds of crocosmia cultivars, and no late summer garden should be without their warmth of colour in shades of yellow, orange and red. The foliage alone is an asset, the tufts of sword-like leaves giving form to planting schemes and remaining fresh from spring to their late summer flowering.

• One great performer is the hardy, vigorous and robust *Crocosmia* 'Emily McKenzie', which has large, burnt orange trumpets streaked with mahogany and grows to a height of 60 cm. It is the shape of the flowering heads that makes crocosmias exceptional. The strong stems arch upwards from the leaves, bearing buds that turn almost horizontal before opening from the bottom into a beak-like shape. The overall impression is of flowers shaped like the head of a tropical bird.

• Crocosmias are cormous perennials, which means they grow from corms that renew themselves by making new corms directly under the old. The new corms will carry next year's shoots and flowers. When sited in a sunny spot with plenty of drainage added to the soil, they will increase rapidly, making a dense clump that may soon become congested and suffer reduced flowering. In this case, the clumps should be lifted and the corms and baby cormels separated out. Replant them, preferably in the autumn, as new shoots are too easily broken off in the spring.

• One of the surprises of crocosmias (commonly known as montbretias) is that, although they like the sun, they will nonetheless grow in partial shade. Some of the other great cultivars to grow are 'Star of the East', which has large apricot-orange flowers, and, most popular of all, fiery red 'Lucifer', which makes an appearance as early as July.

Crocosmia × crocosmiiflora 'Emily McKenzie'

Sedum 'Autumn Joy' Sedums have the advantage of looking good almost all year round. The grey, succulent new foliage is in evidence at the same time as the old, and is revealed once the spent flower-heads have been removed. Becoming slowly fatter as spring and summer progress, the foliage takes on the frosty bloom that gives sedum the name ice plant.

• The grey flower-heads that form in summer are very similar to heads of broccoli, and only gradually assume their true colour. The starry flowers of *Sedum* 'Autumn Joy' (sometimes known as 'Herbstfreude') take on a dark pink hue that gradually turns to a deep russet with the onset of autumn.

• The flower-heads attract hordes of butterflies and many beneficial insects to collect their nectar. Once spent, the flower-heads can be left on the plant to protect the crown throughout the winter, which also allows any overnight frost to enhance their form. Cutting these heads off in late winter or early spring reveals the new growth and the cycle starts again.

• Sedums sometimes have a tendency towards floppiness when the flower-heads are in full flow. This can be remedied by dividing established clumps in the spring, or agitating the roots of the plant with a fork.

The stonecrop or ice plant, as sedum is commonly known, belongs to a family of succulent-leafed sun-lovers whose thick, fleshy leaves act as a sort of moisture store for the plant. They are happy almost anywhere, excellent for dry areas of the garden with poor soil, and almost thrive on neglect.

Canna 'Wyoming'

Although cannas have been out of vogue for a long time, the fan club is swelling because these flowers blend so well with the more 'tropical' planting schemes currently seen in garden centres and nurseries. Cannas have a magnificence of stature, luxuriance of leaf and excitement of flower unmatched by any other plant in September.

• In leaf alone, *Canna* 'Wyoming' earns its keep. The foliage unfurls into paddle shapes with rich purple colouring, blending with and providing a background to ornamental grasses or other sword-shaped leaves, such as those of crocosmias. Towards the end of summer, tall stems appear bearing spiky buds, each one gradually opening to a rich apricot-orange that contrasts startlingly with the leaves. The flower spike opens bud by bud until the top one has been reached.

• 'Wyoming', with a long growing season and optimum growing conditions, can reach a statuesque 1.8 m tall. Like all cannas, it must have lots of organic matter dug into the soil before being planted out in late spring. Liquid fertilizer applied while watering will also be gratefully received and repaid.

• Cannas require the same treatment as dahlias at the end of the season. Allow the foliage to be blackened by frost, then lift the rhizomes and store them in spent compost in a frost-free place with a little water to prevent shrivelling. Pot up the rhizomes in spring and plant them out at the end of May.

Gladiolus callianthus When planted in soldier-like ranks for cutting and exhibition, the colourful, top-heavy blooms of gladioli can look rigid and charmless. Some varieties, however, have a wonderful grace and presence. One of these is *Gladiolus callianthus*.

• Sometimes listed as *Acidanthera bicolor* var. *murielae*, this variety has the stiff, sword-shaped leaves of the gladiolus family, but here they are self-supporting. The stems are arching and graceful, with long buds at the end.

• The striking white flowers open in September and have the delicacy and form of a butterfly. The centre, which is a most unusual deep purple or even chocolate brown, looks like a mirror image of the flower shape. The bonus of *G. callianthus* is the fragrance,

which is powerful and heady on warm days.

• A dozen corms will fill a container 45 cm in diameter, and eventually make a lovely display on a patio. Alternatively, several corms can be grown in small plastic pots, and then planted out to fill gaps in the late summer border.

• As *G. callianthus* is tender, it needs to be planted out in late spring. It should also be lifted and dried off for storage over the winter in a cool, frost-free environment.

'This can be the most productive time to garden'

Salvia patens Around 900 species of salvia or sage exist worldwide, some well known for their culinary uses, others for their colour. Whether perennial, half-hardy or annual, salvias always make a reliable contribution either through foliage or flower.

• For the late summer/early autumn garden the intense royal blue flowers of the Mexican native *Salvia patens* are a must, giving colour through September and into October. Mature plants may reach 75 cm high and spread 60 cm wide, with branching, square stems that are sticky to the touch and hairy, spear-shaped leaves. The flowers are unusual, having a large lower petal with a hooded upper lip, and appear in widely spaced pairs up the length of the stem. They love to be planted in sun and do best in moist, fertile soil.

• *S. patens* is not reliably hardy, although it is treated as a hardy perennial in southern parts of Britain and given a thick mulch for winter protection. A plastic cloche placed over the plant will also aid its survival.

• In colder areas, lifting and storing plants is recommended, as *S. patens* forms tuberous roots and can be treated like dahlias for overwintering (see page 105).

Anemone × hybrida 'Honorine Jobert'

In contrast to the sometimes un-subtle colours of late summer flowers, the Japanese anemone 'Honorine Jobert' has a fresh, pure delicacy and a long flowering season.

• Although Japanese anemones will grow in moist shade or sun, they always look happier in partial shade rather than full sunlight. Planted in a group around a small tree or with a background of shrubs, they will light up a shady corner. 'Honorine Jobert' looks particularly stunning planted between the red stems and white, variegated leaves of *Cornus alba* 'Elegantissima'.

• The simple flower shape of this anemone has 6–9 fluttering white petals surrounding a circle of golden stamens. As it is slow to get into spring growth, bulbs can be planted around it, and the growing foliage of the anemone will conceal any dying leaves of bulbs that have finished their season.

• The dark green foliage spreads to cover an area of 60 cm, and the wiry stems can rise to a height of 1.2 m if the soil is fertile enough. It is said that Japanese anemones will run too freely at the root and pop up everywhere, but 'Honorine Jobert' looks best in an imposing group, and any unwanted plants can easily be removed. Any further propagation can be by division in spring or autumn, or by root cuttings in winter.

• Other interesting varieties include *A. × hybrida* 'Whirlwind', which has semi-double, white flowers, and *A. × h.* 'September Charm', which is silvery pink and a little shorter in height.

Dahlia 'Bishop of Llandaff'   There are some fantastic flower shapes and outrageous colours to choose from among dahlias, but for flower form and foliage 'Bishop of Llandaff' is one to treasure. The flowers are single in form but an intoxicating and glowing scarlet right down to the central ring of golden stamens that encircle the almost black centre. One of the attributes that sets this dahlia apart from others is the attractive foliage, which is dark purple with an almost metallic hue veering towards bronze or pewter.

• Dahlia tubers can be started off into growth in a greenhouse in early spring, and cuttings taken from the sprouting shoots. A greenhouse is not essential, however, and the tubers can be planted directly into the garden in May after enriching the soil with compost. This can make them vulnerable to slugs and snails, so it is better to start them off in pots placed on the patio, where pest control and watering can be readily monitored. Growing them in this way also means that the pots can be placed in gaps left in the garden by other plants.

• Leaving the tubers in the ground over the winter is risky. Better to lift them after late frosts have killed off the tender foliage and turned it black. The soil should be cleaned off and the tubers stored in compost in a shed or garage over the winter, with a very occasional watering to prevent shrivelling.

• Two other dahlias are definitely worth having for their attractive foliage and flowers: 'Ellen Houston' has a dwarf habit (60 cm), burnished bronze leaves and deep orange flowers, while 'David Howard' is taller (1.5 m) with similar leaves but paler orange flowers. An interesting and even taller species (2 m) is *Dahlia merckii*, which has single mauve flowers. It is very hardy if planted deeply in well-drained soil and full sun.

Colchicum autumnale Colchicums are commonly known as naked ladies because their flowers appear without leaves. It is this 'unclothed' appearance that makes them ideally suited for planting through low-growing ground cover. They grow from shiny corms that can be planted as soon as they become available in late summer, and settle best in a sunny spot with fertile, well-drained soil that does not dry out too quickly.

• The lavender-pink chalices of *Colchicum autumnale* will appear within a few weeks of planting. The glossy, strappy leaves will not make an appearance until the following spring, and it is important not to tidy them up until they have faded, for it is these leaves that will nourish the production of autumn flowers before the corms become dormant for the summer. Feeding with a general-purpose fertilizer before the leaves die down will help to improve the quality of the autumn flower display.

• Growing in meadows throughout Europe, *C. autumnale* can be naturalized in lawns by lifting the corms in summer when they are dormant, and separating and replanting any offsets. Other good varieties include *C. speciosum* 'Album' with white flowers, C. 'The Giant' with very large, rosy-lilac flowers and *C. cilicicum* 'Purpureum' with dark purple flowers.

Echinacea purpurea It is September when members of
the daisy family from the prairies of North America show their
horticultural value by taking the garden into the lower light
levels and colours of autumn.

• *Echinacea purpurea* is an upright perennial with hairy stems and leaves that will
grow to an eventual height of 90 cm;
well-fed plants in moisture-rich soil and
full sun will grow even taller. They earn
their keep by exuberantly producing
large, lilac-purple daisies well into
October, and these act as a magnet for
bees and butterflies.

• The name echinacea comes from the
Greek word *echinos*, meaning 'hedgehog'
– clearly a reference to the domed, rusty
brown centre of the plant, which is
prickly to touch.

• These flowers relish well-manured soil
and a sunny patch in the garden. Within
a natural planting scheme they contrast
well with ornamental grasses, or with
purple foliage at their base and soft pink
repeat-flowering roses.

• Dead-heading is essential only for tidy
gardeners, as the spent heads can look
good in late autumn, particularly after
a frost. Big clumps should be divided up
in spring, when an early application of
compost will be appreciated. Root
cuttings can also be taken at this time.

OCTOBER
& NOVEMBER

While the last few chores of autumn are completed, there is time for **quiet reflection** on the highlights of the gardening year.

As leaves start to fall, the luxuriant textures of bark come into focus and a multitude of colourful **berries** emerges. Among these are the plump hips of *Rosa moyesii*, which replace its summer flowers and confirm the arrival of autumn.

Although there are fewer plants to choose from at this time of year, our selections are coveted nonetheless for their **remarkable** range and form. The elegance of *Aconitum carmichaelii* 'Arendsii' adds a haze of lofty blue, while *Nerine bowdenii* shimmers like a pink firework. *Cyclamen hederifolium* is just starting to emerge, and myriad colourful chrysanthemums will flower well into December. The garden is having its **final fling** before winter sets in.

As *Gardeners' World* comes to an end, we are already planning for the future. If you've read this far, you may already have decided which plants to treat yourself to for each month next year. The gardening business is a highly tuned industry and very successful at predicting trends, as well as setting them. New varieties of seed, bulb or plant, which may have been up to 10 years in development, are launched every day of the week. Thanks to the skill of dedicated horticulturalists, these will grow taller, fatter or straighter, appear in a variety of new colours, be resistant to pests and diseases, and tolerant of many gardening situations. As the latest brochures constantly prove, we've never had so much to choose from.

This is the **perfect time** to take stock of your garden and sow the seeds of ideas for next year.

Aconitum carmichaelii 'Arendsii' Just when you thought the garden was finished for the year, the tall spikes of *Aconitum carmichaelii* 'Arendsii' start to open, providing the height and colour previously supplied by their delphinium relatives.

• 'Arendsii' is a misleading plant. Its habit of making the foliage start to die back and turn yellow can lead the gardener to think the plant is on the way out, but then flowering begins and blue hooded blooms appear on spikes that tower 1.2 m or more above the border.

• Aconites grow from tubers, which tend to become congested after two or three years, so they will need dividing and replanting. This is best carried out in the autumn, after flowering, planting back only the most vigorous and largest tubers, as aconites get started very early: new growth from the base of plants may be visible in January. They go on to develop into rich green clumps of deeply divided, weed-smothering foliage.

• Aconites are very hardy and adaptable, growing in damp soil and shade, as well as in sun, but responding to a mulch in the spring. Earlier-flowering varieties include *Aconitum × cammarum* 'Bicolor' with blue-and-white flowers in July, and the August-flowering, indigo-blue 'Spark's Variety'.

Schizostylis coccinea The hardy and adaptable *Schizostylis coccinea* is a great 'filler', growing from thin rhizomes that rapidly increase to form thickets of fresh and bright green leaf blades. At flowering time the plant's slender stalks are covered in tight buds. These erupt from the bottom upwards into a profusion of coral-red, star-shaped blooms, each one with a satiny sheen and each stalk carrying numerous individual flowers. A clump will grow to a manageable height of 45 cm and never need staking, but if the soil is too dry, it will not flower. This plant likes lots of sun and moisture, even growing in shallow water.

• Frequent splitting is needed to encourage a good show of flowers: do this every couple of years, or even every year if growth has been good. This makes the crimson flag a bargain plant as small divisions quickly grow into generous colonies. These look good towards the front of a border, drifting through other plants and contrasting particularly well with the purple foliage of the ground cover *Heuchera* 'Palace Purple' and ornamental grasses.

• Among the cultivars available are 'Major', which has larger, red flowers, 'Mrs Hegarty', which is a bright, clear pink, and 'Sunrise', which is salmon pink.

Originally from South Africa, the crimson flag (as *Schizostylis coccinea* is commonly known) is worth growing in any garden, for it opens its cheerful flowers at the onset of autumn and often continues into December, regardless of the weather. It is among the last flowers of the season, the spikes of blossom looking like a very late gladiolus, but the crimson flag is a relative of the iris, having the familiar sword-shaped and upright leaves of that family.

Cyclamen hederifolium The unusual flowering and fabulous foliage of *Cyclamen hederifolium* make it one of the most useful plants. The story starts in the autumn, when myriad delicate but beautifully formed, long-petalled flowers appear in varying shades of pink and white.

• The foliage, similar to that of ivy (hence the name *hederifolium*), follows the flowers. Basically dark green, the leaves are marbled with silver and grey-green towards the edges and carpet the ground where the flowers have been. The foliage remains as ground cover throughout the winter and into the spring.
• In the spring the foliage disappears and the tubers become dormant for the whole of the summer, leaving a gap in beds and borders. It is therefore useful to mix plantings of cyclamen with other shade-tolerant plants, such as ferns, which will cover but not smother the ground in summer.
• *C. hederifolium* grows wild in the woods of southern Europe, and is most at home in the shade of trees and shrubs. Although it can tolerate very dry conditions when the leaf canopy opens and prevents moisture reaching the soil, cyclamen tubers dislike total dehydration, so a mulch in spring will help to preserve moisture.
• Established tubers can become as large as dinner plates, and in early spring little seedlings with tiny, pearl-sized tubers can be found in the centre of them. These can be moved and transplanted in the vicinity to help with the colonization process.

> The garden
> is having its
> final fling
> before winter
> sets in

■ *Nerine bowdenii* The flowering of *Nerine bowdenii* is affected by moisture in the soil, so dewy autumnal mornings often trigger the appearance of the plant's lily-like trumpets in round clusters on top of leafless stems. The firework display of bright pink flowers starts in October, when the petals, covered with tiny, pearl-like cells, glisten and sparkle in the light. Flowers last for a long time, making them good for cutting, and sometimes carry on well into November when left outside.

• Nerines are hardy in all but the coldest and wettest of winters, the flowers surviving any amount of frost in autumn. The strappy leaves of *N. bowdenii* are nearly withered away before the flowers appear. The plants need feeding with a general-purpose fertilizer while growing and before becoming dormant.

• Planting is recommended in late summer, preferably against warm walls or in sheltered places with full sun. The snouts of the bulbs should be placed at soil level so that they get a good baking in the summer to flower freely. They need a very free-draining soil to prevent waterlogging in the winter.

• Nerines can be grown in containers in gritty compost, and may flower all the better for a bit of congestion. The bulbs should be split up only when dormant in the summer and when the pots are bulging.

Rosa moyesii Brought back from western China in 1905 by the plant hunter E.H. Wilson and introduced into cultivation in 1908, *Rosa moyesii* is a large, arching shrub needing plenty of room. The form 'Geranium', which was raised at Wisley in 1938, is more compact, growing to a height of 2 m. *R. moyesii* has two seasons of interest, but its main value in the garden is its autumnal display.

• In midsummer, *R. moyesii* smothers its leafy branches with blazing red, single flowers, each one 5 cm across with bright yellow stamens. Once flowering is finished, the bush should be left untouched because the spent flowers will gradually transform into hips. In fact, it is for its magnificent display of curvaceous, dangling hips that this rose is mainly grown, for with the onset of autumn the glossy fruits clothe the bush once again in vermilion.

• 'Geranium' is a species rose and needs very little pruning, apart from tipping back any overlong stems. An established shrub may need dead, diseased and damaged wood removed, as well as a bit of reshaping, and this should be done when the plant is dormant in winter. Very old stems carrying multitudes of weak branches can be cut out at the same time. As shrub roses flower on older wood, any over-zealous cutting back will result in very few flowers and, consequently, no fruits the following year.

• Good, rich soil and feeding are paramount for the health and vigour of roses, so a yearly application of manure or a thick mulch will give plants a tonic.

Chrysanthemum In blazing shades of gold, bronze, yellow, orange, pink and red, chrysanthemums are the epitome of autumn flowers, needing longer hours of darkness to trigger them into bloom. The Chinese were growing chrysanthemums for medicinal and ornamental purposes 2500 years ago, but it was not until the end of the eighteenth century that they arrived in Europe.

• There are many classifications and groups that describe the flower shape, size and season, but this information can be ignored by ordinary gardeners. It is sufficient to know that chrysanthemums can fill the garden with colour from October to December and provide rich pickings for the house.

• 'Emperor of China' is a very old variety that grows up to 1.2 m tall, so it needs support. The pink blooms have quilled petals and are formed in loose sprays over the foliage that gives a bonus of crimson veining as the autumn progresses. A slightly smaller pink variety is 'Mei-Kyo', which has double flowers that stand up well to the weather.

'Pennine Oriel' is tall but with single, creamy flowers, while 'Nantyderry Sunshine' is a brilliant yellow.

• Given rich soil and reasonable moisture, chrysanthemums are easy to grow, but they must not be overfed or they will become lanky and more susceptible to disease. Plant them in full sun out of any frost pockets and they will flower well in a cold autumn. Support is needed for the taller varieties, but they can be cut back in June to make more compact, sturdier plants. They quickly form large clumps that should be lifted and divided in early spring. A few cuttings taken from the base of the plant will root quickly and be ready for planting out in May.

Aster × frikartii 'Mönch' Perennial asters are commonly known in Britain as Michaelmas daisies because their flowering coincides with the feast of St Michael on 29 September. Although some asters may open their flowers earlier, their peak of bloom starts at the end of September and runs through October until the first frosts.

• If there is room for only one aster in your garden, make sure it is *Aster × frikartii* 'Mönch'. This not only has a very long flowering season – from late summer well into October – but is also one of the most mildew-resistant varieties.

• The Greek word *aster* means 'star', and these flowers live up to their name. The lavender-blue petals are like rays, opening out flat around a sunshine-yellow centre. The modestly proportioned 'Mönch' has an upright habit and freely branching stems, which grow to 90 cm. Asters are very attractive to bees and butterflies because varieties producing seed-heads

are a valuable source of winter food for birds. The plants like well-drained soil in full sun, and prefer not to be overcrowded. A mulch in spring and, if the summer has been hot, watering towards the end of summer and into autumn will keep the plants healthy. Overcrowded clumps can be divided in either autumn or spring, and cuttings taken from the base of a clump in the spring will root quickly.

• Other varieties with good mildew resistance are *A. amellus* 'King George' and *A. divaricatus*. The latter has clouds of white flowers, rather like gypsophila.

DECEMBER & JANUARY

December and January are the quiet months, and the winter garden has its own unique atmosphere. Bare-leafed branches are starkly silhouetted against leaden skies and colour is something of a rarity. Don't despair: there are plants to brighten even the dullest day, and these will become the cherished jewels of your winter garden.

These months are all about early debuts. Flowers that make their best displays in winter are as tough as old boots. Frost, rain, snow, nothing will stop the efforts of say, *Cyclamen coum*, which not only flourishes in the coldest conditions but multiplies year by year to carpet the ground.

At this time other plants are like time capsules, lying dormant while storing up the makings of their flowers. Tightly curled yet perfectly formed leaves are waiting for water, the right temperature and increasing daylight to give them the kick start they need. It's amazing to think that plants have their own internal biological clock and that some choose to weather the winter.

If you are yet to become a fully hardy gardener – willing to step outside whatever the weather – then it is worth planting these rare winter flowers where they can be enjoyed from indoors. A haze of cyclamen viewed from the kitchen sink keeps the garden in your sights and in your mind. Opening the curtains to reveal a carpet of winter aconites in low light is an excuse to linger with that first hot drink of the day.

This is a time of year when seasoned gardeners look ahead. What hasn't been achieved last year will surely happen next: this border will be bolder, that tired corner will be rejuvenated… Expert or novice, all gardeners are optimistic. Whichever you might be, happy new year to you and your garden – the fun has only just begun.

■ *Clematis cirrhosa* 'Freckles' Just when it seems that everything in the garden has gone to sleep, *Clematis cirrhosa* 'Freckles' wakes up and opens its nodding flower-heads. These are a creamy pink colour densely speckled with red and crimson, and have prominent yellow stamens at the centre. The main crop of flowers starts before the real grip of winter, but flowering continues intermittently during mild spells.

• In harsh climates, this clematis can be grown in the shelter of a conservatory. If grown outside, choose a sheltered aspect, or you will need to provide protection against frost. For the joy of having flowers during this bare season, the extra effort is worth it.

• Placed in a sunny site near a sheltered south or southwest-facing wall, 'Freckles' will grow to a height of 3–4 m, covering the surface with dark green, glossy leaves larger than those of the species plant.

• Like all clematis, it appreciates lots of manure on planting, and liquid feeding when in active growth until flowering starts. Pruning is simple, merely requiring dead or weak stems to be removed after flowering.

Helleborus argutifolius On a frosty January morning the subtle, pale green buds of *Helleborus argutifolius* hang their ice-coated heads as if clustered together for warmth. This, however, is their flowering habit and belies their robust nature.

• Known as the Corsican hellebore after its place of origin, *H. argutifolius* is an evergreen tough guy, growing vigorously in any fertile soil in sun or part shade to the size of a small shrub. The flowers will not fade or drop off the plant, but last for weeks, protecting the ripening seed within.

• This hellebore is worth growing for its foliage alone. In their first year of planting the semi-woody stems bear trifoliate leaves, each one margined with 'mock' prickles. The leaves are leathery to the touch, sea green in colour and netted with grey veins and a 'dot' of red where each leaf joins the stem. In the second year stout clusters of pale green buds open to nodding cups of jade.

• Don't be too hasty to cut off the flowers of hellebores because the plants can be short-lived and may need to be replaced. The seeds should be allowed to drop and germinate or be collected. It is said that the seed is also distributed by slugs and snails, which eat the coating and carry the seed away on their slime, thus distributing it around the garden.

• Hellebores will relish a thick mulching with leaf mould or spent mushroom compost in July and August when the new flower-buds are being formed. This can be repeated in December, when any blackened or tatty foliage can be removed to make the plants pristine and ready to show off their winter blooms.

Iris unguicularis In the depths of winter, gardening is about small treasures, fleeting scents and surprises, and *Iris unguicularis* is all of these.

• The narrow, evergreen foliage arises from wiry rhizomes, eventually forming untidy clumps about 30 cm tall. This untidiness is quickly pardoned, for sometimes as early as Christmas a little searching among the leaves will reveal the formation of buds. From then on, a daily trip outdoors is essential to check on their progress.

• Once buds look ready to break open, pick them carefully, as they form in pairs and pulling may destroy a developing bud. Bring them indoors and watch them unfurl their silky-textured, almost crystalline, mauve petals to reveal their beautifully netted central markings, and inhale their sweet fragrance from the comfort of an armchair. Flowers will last for two or three days.

• The Algerian iris grows in many Mediterranean areas, so in the garden choose the hottest and sunniest position for it at the base of a south-facing wall. It can be planted in the driest of soils, needing little care apart from an autumnal grooming of the leaves to remove dead foliage and any snails that may have taken up residence.

• Good varieties of *I. unguicularis* are 'Walter Butt', with very pale mauve flowers, and 'Mary Barnard' (left), which is a deeper violet.

▲ *Eranthis hyemalis* Tubers of winter aconite are best planted under deciduous trees and shrubs where they are unlikely to be disturbed. Here they can benefit from partial shade and moisture during the summer months, but can make the most of any sunshine during the winter.

• Their bright green leaves poke 5–10 cm out of the ground and make a divided collar or ruff around the flower that opens from their centre. Each plant spreads to only 8 cm, but will self-seed once established, the seed ripening in early May.

• In the first year after germinating, nothing but a pair of shiny seed leaves appears. These can easily be mistaken for weeds, but it is best to give them the benefit of the doubt and let them grow

on. In the second year a circular leaf grows, and in the third year the first flower appears.

• Like most winter-flowering plants, aconites respond well to being mulched after flowering. This will retain enough moisture in the ground to keep them happy over the summer months. Winter aconites also respond well to being divided and moved 'in the green' – that is immediately after flowering while the leaves are still visible.

A colony of winter aconites is worth the patience needed to establish them, for a bright carpet of buttercup-yellow cups is one of the most welcoming sights in the winter garden. It is the thin January sunshine that prompts the opening of their flowers, and this has led to their other common name, New Year's gift.

Adonis amurensis For very early flowers in a sunny spot,
alpine bed or front of a border, *Adonis amurensis* is a serious rival
to the winter aconite.

• A native of mountain meadows in
Japan and Korea, the adonis is an ultra-
hardy perennial that prefers well-drained
(but not poor) soil, moisture and a bit
of shelter in a partially shaded spot. Here
it can put down its fibrous roots before
sending out clumps of glistening, very
finely divided, lacy foliage.

• The bowl-shaped flowers, 5 cm across,
appear in January on small clumps of
leafy stems. They are bright yellow with
a green tinge, and the underside is tinted
bronze. Flowering on established plants
can continue into March before the plant
dies down. This makes the adonis a good
companion for spreading perennials,
such as hardy geraniums, which will fill
the gap over the summer months.

• Adonis plants are often a pleasant
surprise because they tend to be
forgotten, unless the planting site
has been marked. After flowering,
they completely disappear into their
dormancy for the length of the summer
through to late autumn.

• Division or re-siting of clumps should
be done during the dormancy period,
which is a good reason for labelling them
– they can be easily found and not dug
up by mistake.

■ *Cyclamen coum* In a daring act of defiance to winter weather, *Cyclamen coum* throws out its flowers in shades of magenta, pink or white from as early as Christmas and continues right through to March.

• It thrives in one of the most difficult garden positions – in rooty soil around the base of trees. Here it can have light shade during the summer, but it needs moisture from the autumn to late spring. As cyclamens can take a long time to establish if planted as dry tubers, it may be worth buying plants already in flower; these always seem to establish more quickly.

• Once settled and undisturbed, *C. coum* will rapidly expand to form a colony. The number of flowers will increase year by year as the tubers become larger and larger, and seedlings will start to appear as if by magic. (This is thanks to seed being borne away by ants.)

• Cyclamens can be successfully grown in troughs, along north-facing walls and in rock gardens. In the summer, when dormant, a top-dressing of leaf mould will keep the tubers just moist and raring to go into their winter display.

'There are plants to brighten even the dullest day'

FEBRUARY

February is the starting point for *Gardeners' World*, the beginning of 36 programmes that take us through the changing seasons of the gardening year. In all likelihood, the opening shot of the very first programme will be a breathtaking view of one of the flowers appearing in this chapter. This is a moment of great optimism and enthusiasm for everyone working on the series because one shot, and we know we have you hooked.

Plants that succeed in February are undoubtedly among the stars of the gardening year. It is easy, for example, to become fascinated by snowdrops for, warmed by winter sunshine, the tiny white bells open and release their delicate honey fragrance. The urge to kneel down and marvel at the markings within becomes irresistible. Vast quantities of money can change hands for just one snowdrop bulb if the flower has unusual markings.

On *Gardeners' World* we are all addicted to hellebores, and expeditions to hunt out new contributors for the programme always seem to lead us to the hellebore grower. If we have a tendency to revel in this plant every year, we can only say that it remains endlessly rewarding.

We can't pretend that searching out flowers for this time of year is easy, and it does mean we have yielded to one shrub – the camellia. It just had to be included for its potent perfection.

February is a time of year when gardeners can get impatient: the ground is hard and unworkable, and the weather unreliable. If the flowers we've chosen are brave enough to endure the bleak days of winter, we should celebrate their beauty for as long as possible.

▲ *Camellia × williamsii* 'Debbie' When given the right growing conditions, camellias are tough and easy-going shrubs with glossy, evergreen leaves and a diverse array of flower shapes, which all have the carved look of confectionery decorations.

• Camellias are available in literally hundreds of varieties, so it's best to make your selection when they are in bloom, as form, flower and colour can be more easily assessed. While *Camellia × williamsii* hybrids may not have the diversity of *C. japonica*, they are hard to beat for hardiness and free-flowering.

• 'Debbie' has been in cultivation since 1965 and has proved to be one of the most popular varieties. The sheer flamboyance of its clear pink petal masses that form the peony-shaped, stemless blooms against a backdrop of dark green, glossy leaves gives a tropical air to a winter's day.

• All that camellias need to thrive is a leafy, acid soil, a bit of shade and a situation that never faces the morning sun, for their flower buds will be scorched if they have been caught by an overnight frost. They will benefit from organic matter being dug into the ground before they are planted, and appreciate having a mulch around their base in late summer. No pruning is required; simply shape occasionally and remove any dead flower-heads.

• For gardeners without acid soil, camellias will grow well in containers filled with ericaceous compost, but they must be well watered and fed during the summer months to ensure good flower-bud formation.

Crocus tommasinianus 'Whitewell Purple'

Crocuses are just made for planting in large drifts, and luckily the small corms are inexpensive to buy in late summer, so an immediate effect is easily achievable.

• *Crocus tommasinianus*, of which 'Whitewell Purple' is a variety, will grow to a height of 10 cm and is also willing to seed itself about, spreading into large drifts, which look best under deciduous shrubs, or naturalized in grass where their leaves will be reasonably disguised. The slender, purple buds of 'Whitewell Purple' emerge through the foliage early in the month, opening to reveal silver-mauve insides and bright orange stamens.

• Many crocus species come from countries bordering the Mediterranean and are not suited to shady spots. Provided they have sun and preferably gritty, well-drained soil, they will flourish. However, they will close up and remain firmly shut on dull and rainy days.

• As with all bulbs, plant crocuses at about twice their depth (7 cm) and 3 cm apart. Once in the ground, they need no special care. After flowering, scatter some general-purpose fertilizer over them and allow the flowers and leaves to die down naturally; in borders the emerging growth of other perennials makes rapid cover. Naturalized bulbs in grass can have the dead foliage mown off in late spring, which allows time for the corms to build up food reserves from the leaves before going into summer dormancy.

• Overcrowding can be remedied by lifting clumps as the leaves turn brown, separating the corms and cormlets, and replanting.

Iris 'Katharine Hodgkin' There are many varieties of dwarf bulbous iris, all primed and ready to push their delicate and bright blooms through the cold winter earth. All you need is a well-drained patch of soil in a sunny place.

• The reliable and lovely 'Katharine Hodgkin' has pale blue alabaster flowers streaked with veins of mauve, and its falls are marked with black and lemon around a central streak of saffron. It is vigorous, easy to grow and lends itself to planting in pots, where its exquisite nature can be closely appreciated.

• Other varieties worth considering are *Iris histrioides*, whose deep blue flowers with yellow-and-white-splashed falls sometimes appear as early as January, and *I. reticulata*, which appears soon after in shades of blue through to dark purple. Being just 10–15 cm tall, dwarf irises are best grown in clumps: in fact, a massed effect is essential for enjoyment of plants that are so small. They make ideal container plants, kept near the house while in flower, then placed out of sight once flowering is over. Bulbs potted up in plastic pots can be plunged

(i.e. planted pot and all) in borders temporarily, then taken away so that the foliage can die down out of sight.

• Some dwarf irises have an annoying habit of disappearing after flowering. This happens when the bulb breaks down into dozens of tiny bulblets, which will take years to reach flowering size. *I. danfordiae* is a prime example of this, so buy it fresh every year. Its very early, bright yellow flowers make it worth the outlay.

◩ *Helleborus orientalis* **hybrids**   The Lenten rose was introduced in the nineteenth century and is named after its period of flowering, which runs from late winter to early spring. Its promiscuous nature, as well as selective breeding by keen plantspeople, has produced an overwhelming choice of flower colours, from white to nearly black, and a variety of flower forms, from saucer-shaped and outward-facing to nodding and double-flowered.

• Hellebores like cool conditions and moisture, thriving, if well mulched, under trees and among shrubs in partial shade. They look their best in a part-shady border alongside snowdrops or the emerging foliage of later-flowering herbaceous perennials.

• The flowers linger on hellebores for a long time, but once the seed has been collected or dispersed from them, the stalks can be cut to the ground. *Helleborus orientalis* will often seed itself about, so you will find many new and interesting seedlings to grow on.

• Old leaves often begin to look tatty around flowering time, and it does no harm to cut them off. The new leaves quickly emerge along with the flowering stems, giving a fresh look to each plant. Special treasures can be divided, and this is best carried out just after or even during flowering, making sure that the newly planted divisions are kept moist to re-establish them well.

There are few better sights in winter than a group of *H. orientalis* in full flower, and no better pastime than to lift their heads and stare into their remarkable centres. The contrast between the flower colour, stamens and inner speckling is simply enchanting.

▲ *Hepatica transsilvanica* Hepaticas are members of the buttercup family and are found throughout Europe, Asia and North America. They are among the first flowers of early spring, appearing during mild spells in the leaf litter on woodland slopes in their native habitat.

• On a bright day, the many single flowers open wide in shades of blue, pink and white, their stamen colours ranging from white, cream and pink to blue, red and even green. Some varieties have a delicate fragrance.

• *Hepatica transsilvanica* is best planted under deciduous trees or shrubs with lots of leaf mould and grit added to the soil. There its bright blue, starry flowers will appear in quantity before the new foliage. This species spreads by creeping rhizomes, and is one of the more robust and vigorous hepaticas. The first leaves of the year, glossy and bright green, start to unfurl in February, making a shiny carpet of ground cover that persists throughout the summer months.

• Many other good hepaticas are available, some with very decorative leaf forms.

Certain varieties of *H. nobilis*, for example, have marbled foliage, while some of the cultivated Japanese forms have double flowers.

• All hepaticas like to be planted in shady positions, even in the rock garden. They need little aftercare, other than the removal of old leaves just before flowering, a top-dressing of leaf mould in the autumn and a scattering of fish, blood and bone in late winter.

Galanthus 'S. Arnott' One of the finest cultivars around, *Galanthus* 'S. Arnott' grows larger than the norm, up to 25 cm, and has large, well-rounded flowers that are sturdy, well proportioned and powerfully scented (lots aren't). Its display is extended because it opens its buds in succession. Once established, a clump will rapidly expand, but may become congested, resulting in a poor display. To avoid this, lift, divide and replant once flowering has finished.

• Although not native to the United Kingdom, snowdrops have been with us since medieval times and are completely at home in our woodlands. They naturally like to carpet the ground on banks, in hedgerows and under trees, so it makes sense to grow them in similar garden spots where they can be undisturbed. Plant them in soil that is fertile and not too dry.

• Snowdrops can be difficult to establish from bulbs, so it is recommended that they are bought 'in the green' – that is, with their leaves on. Once started, they need little further attention. Specialist nurseries have many different varieties, while garden centres offer a limited range, but sell them in small pots for planting out in flower.

Calendar of 1000 Flowering Plants

Any of our 100 flowers of the moment will make a special addition to your garden (and they are shown in **bold** type in the list below), but there are literally hundreds of other plants to choose from. This section is a list of 1000 fantastic flowers, including perennials, climbers, bulbs and annuals. It has been arranged according to the month of flowering, colour, cultivation requirements, height and spread.

By choosing plants from this list that suit your own colour palette as well as the particular conditions in your garden, you can create a harmonious space that will give you colour throughout the seasons.

calendar of flowering plants & index

spring: march

latin name	common name	flowering	sun/shade	moisture	height	spread
Pulmonaria rubra	Lungwort	Mar–May	partial shade	moist	30 cm	30 cm
Tulipa 'Giuseppe Verdi'	Tulip	Mar–Apr	sun	well-drained	30 cm	15 cm
Epimedium × warleyense p.17	Barrenwort	Mar–May	sun/partial shade	moist	30 cm	30 cm
Narcissus 'Jet Fire'	Daffodil	Mar–Apr	sun	well-drained	25 cm	10 cm
Caltha palustris p.16	Marsh marigold	Mar–May	sun	wet	30 cm	45 cm
Epimedium perralderianum	Barrenwort	Mar–May	sun/partial shade	moist	30 cm	30 cm
Epimedium pinnatum subsp. *colchicum*	Barrenwort	Mar–May	sun/partial shade	moist	30 cm	30 cm
Euphorbia characias subsp. *wulfenii*	Spurge	Mar–May	sun	well-drained	1.2 m	90 cm
Euphorbia amygdaloides var. *robbiae*	Spurge	Mar–May	shade	dry	50 cm	50 cm
Narcissus 'Baby Moon'	Daffodil	Mar–Apr	sun	well-drained	25 cm	7 cm
Narcissus bulbocodium	Hoop petticoat daffodil	Mar–Apr	sun	well-drained	15 cm	5 cm
Narcissus cyclamineus	Daffodil	Mar–Apr	sun	well-drained	20 cm	8 cm
Narcissus 'Jenny'	Daffodil	Mar–Apr	sun	well-drained	30 cm	8 cm
Narcissus 'Little Witch'	Daffodil	Mar–Apr	sun	well-drained	20 cm	8 cm
Narcissus 'St Patrick's Day'	Daffodil	Mar–Apr	sun	well-drained	40 cm	15 cm
Epimedium × versicolor 'Sulphureum'	Barrenwort	Mar–May	sun/partial shade	moist	30 cm	30 cm
Helleborus × sternii	Hellebore	Mar–May	sun	well-drained	40 cm	40 cm
Anemone blanda Blue Shades	Windflower	Mar–Apr	partial shade	well-drained	12.5 cm	25 cm
Anemone nemorosa 'Robinsoniana'	Wood anemone	Mar–Apr	shade	moist	15 cm	25 cm
Chionodoxa forbesii 'Blue Giant'	Glory of the snow	Mar–Apr	sun	well-drained	15 cm	5 cm
Chionodoxa luciliae p.15	Glory of the snow	Mar–Apr	sun	well-drained	15 cm	5 cm
Chionodoxa sardensis	Glory of the snow	Mar–Apr	sun	well-drained	15 cm	5 cm
Muscari armeniacum pp20–1	Grape hyacinth	Mar–Apr	sun	well-drained	15 cm	5 cm
Pulmonaria angustifolia 'Munstead Blue'	Lungwort	Mar–May	partial shade	moist	15 cm	30 cm
Scilla siberica	Siberian squill	Mar–Apr	sun/partial shade	well-drained	12 cm	5 cm
Vinca major 'Variegata'	Periwinkle	Mar–May	shade	dry	30 cm	90 cm
Bellis perennis 'Kito Cherry Pink'	Daisy	Mar–May	sun/partial shade	well-drained	15 cm	15 cm
Epimedium grandiflorum 'Rose Queen'	Barrenwort	Mar–May	sun/partial shade	moist	20 cm	20 cm
Epimedium × rubrum	Barrenwort	Mar–May	sun/partial shade	moist	20 cm	20 cm
Bellis perennis 'Goliath'	Daisy	Mar–May	sun/partial shade	well-drained	20 cm	20 cm
Bergenia purpurascens	Elephant's ears	Mar–May	sun/shade	any	30 cm	30 cm
Chionodoxa forbesii 'Pink Giant'	Glory of the snow	Mar–Apr	sun	well-drained	15 cm	5 cm
Corydalis solida 'George Baker'	Corydalis	Mar–May	partial shade	well-drained/moist	30 cm	20 cm
Viola odorata	Violet	Mar–Apr	sun/partial shade	well-drained	15 cm	30 cm
Anemone blanda p.14	Windflower	Mar–Apr	partial shade	well-drained	12.5 cm	25 cm
Anemone blanda 'White Splendour'	Windflower	Mar–Apr	partial shade	well-drained	12.5 cm	25 cm
Anemone nemorosa	Wood anemone	Mar–Apr	shade	moist	15 cm	25 cm
***Bergenia* 'Bressingham White'** p.19	Elephant's ears	Mar–May	sun/shade	any	30 cm	30 cm
Bergenia 'Silberlicht'	Elephant's ears	Mar–May	sun/shade	any	30 cm	30 cm
Caltha palustris var. *alba*	Marsh marigold	Mar–May	sun	wet	15 cm	45 cm
Epimedium × youngianum 'Niveum'	Barrenwort	Mar–May	sun/partial shade	moist	20 cm	20 cm
Muscari botryoides 'Album'	Grape hyacinth	Mar–Apr	sun	well-drained	15 cm	5 cm
***Pulmonaria* 'Sissinghurst White'** p.18	Lungwort	Mar–May	partial shade	moist	25 cm	45 cm
Scilla siberica 'Alba'	Siberian squill	Mar–Apr	sun/partial shade	well-drained	12 cm	5 cm
Vinca minor f. *alba*	Lesser periwinkle	Mar–May	shade	dry	15 cm	90 cm
Hepatica acutiloba	Hepatica	Mar–Jun	partial shade	moist	10 cm	20 cm

spring: april

latin name	common name	flowering	sun/shade	moisture	height	spread
Anthriscus sylvestris 'Ravenswing'	Cow parsley	Apr–May	partial shade	well-drained	1 m	30 cm
Euphorbia dulcis 'Chameleon'	Spurge	Apr–Jul	sun	well-drained	20 cm	20 cm
Trillium sessile	Wake robin	Apr–Jun	shade	well-drained/moist	30 cm	30 cm
Clematis alpina 'Ruby'	Clematis	Apr–May	sun	well-drained	1.8 m	spreading

latin name	common name	flowering	sun/shade	moisture	height	spread
Dicentra 'Bacchanal'	Bleeding heart	Apr–May	partial shade	moist	30 cm	25 cm
Erysimum cheiri 'Blood Red'	Wallflower	Apr–May	sun	well-drained	45 cm	30 cm
Tulipa clusiana 'Cynthia'	Tulip	Apr–May	sun	well-drained	25 cm	10 cm
Tulipa praestans 'Fusilier'	Tulip	Apr–May	sun	well-drained	35 cm	15 cm
Tulipa 'Red Riding Hood'	Tulip	Apr–May	sun	well-drained	30 cm	15 cm
Euphorbia griffithii 'Dixter' p.28	Spurge	Apr–May	sun	well-drained	1 m	60 cm
Fritillaria imperialis 'Aurora'	Crown imperial	Apr–May	sun/partial shade	well-drained/moist	90 cm	45 cm
Tulipa orphanidea Whittallii Group	Tulip	Apr–May	sun	well-drained	30 cm	15 cm
Tulipa 'Prinses Irene'	Tulip	Apr–May	sun	well-drained	30 cm	15 cm
Viola 'Penny Sunrise'	Viola	Apr–July	sun/partial shade	well-drained	15 cm	15 cm
Doronicum × excelsum 'Harpur Crewe'	Leopard's bane	Apr–Jun	partial shade	moist	90 cm	60 cm
Doronicum 'Miss Mason'	Leopard's bane	Apr–Jun	partial shade	moist	45 cm	60 cm
Doronicum pardalianches	Leopard's bane	Apr–Jun	partial shade	moist	75 cm	60 cm
Erysimum cheiri 'Cloth of Gold'	Wallflower	Apr–May	sun	well-drained	35 cm	30 cm
Erythronium 'Pagoda'	Dog's tooth violet	Apr–May	partial shade	moist	25 cm	15 cm
Euphorbia amygdaloides 'Purpurea'	Wood spurge	Apr–May	sun	well-drained	30 cm	30 cm
Euphorbia mellifera	Honey spurge	Apr–May	sun	well-drained	2.4 m	1.2 m
Euphorbia polychroma	Spurge	Apr–May	sun	well-drained	50 cm	50 cm
Fritillaria imperialis 'Lutea'	Crown imperial	Apr–May	sun/partial shade	well-drained/moist	90 cm	45 cm
Lamium galeobdolon 'Florentinum'	Yellow dead nettle	Apr–Jul	shade	moist	15 cm	30 cm
Narcissus 'Hawera'	Daffodil	Apr–May	sun	well-drained	18 cm	8 cm
Uvularia grandiflora	Merrybells	Apr–Jun	partial shade	moist	60 cm	25 cm
Hyacinthus orientalis 'City of Haarlem'	Hyacinth	Apr–May	sun	well-drained	20 cm	10 cm
Narcissus 'Pipit'	Daffodil	Apr–May	sun	well-drained	30 cm	7 cm
Narcissus 'Yellow Cheerfulness'	Daffodil	Apr–May	sun	well-drained	40 cm	15 cm
Primula vulgaris p.29	Primrose	Mar–Apr	sun/partial shade	well-drained/moist	8 cm	13 cm
Gladiolus tristis	Gladiolus	Apr–May	sun	well-drained	90 cm	20 cm
Fritillaria pontica	Fritillary	Apr–May	sun/partial shade	well-drained	30 cm	10 cm
Brunnera macrophylla p.33	Brunnera	Apr–Jun	shade	moist	40 cm	60 cm
Brunnera macrophylla 'Hadspen Cream'	Brunnera	May–Jun	shade	moist	35 cm	60 cm
Clematis alpina 'Frances Rivis'	Clematis	Apr–May	sun	well-drained	1.8 m	spreading
Corydalis flexuosa 'Père David' p.24	Corydalis	Apr–May	partial shade	well-drained/moist	30 cm	20 cm
Hyacinthus orientalis 'Delft Blue'	Hyacinth	Apr–May	sun	well-drained	20 cm	10 cm
Myosotis alpestris 'Blue Ball'	Forget-me-not	Apr–May	sun/partial shade	well-drained/moist	25 cm	25 cm
Scilla peruviana	Squill	Apr–May	sun/partial shade	well-drained	20 cm	15 cm
Viola 'Blue Bird'	Viola	Apr–July	sun/partial shade	well-drained	15 cm	45 cm
Viola sororia	Sister violet	Apr–June	sun/partial shade	well-drained	15 cm	15 cm
Clematis macropetala	Clematis	Apr–May	sun	well-drained	1.8 m	spreading
Corydalis flexuosa 'China Blue'	Corydalis	Apr–May	partial shade	well-drained/moist	30 cm	20 cm
Mertensia pulmonarioides	Virginia cowslip	Apr–May	partial shade	well-drained	45 cm	30 cm
Puschkinia scilloides	Striped squill	Mar–Apr	sun	well-drained	15 cm	2.5 cm
Clematis macropetala 'Markham's Pink'	Clematis	Apr–May	sun	well-drained	1.8 m	spreading
Dicentra formosa	Bleeding heart	Apr–May	partial shade	moist	30 cm	25 cm
Erythronium dens-canis	Dog's tooth violet	Apr–May	partial shade	moist	12 cm	10 cm
Hyacinthus orientalis 'Lady Derby'	Hyacinth	Apr–May	sun	well-drained	20 cm	10 cm
Lamium maculatum 'Beacon Silver'	Dead nettle	Apr–Jul	shade	moist	15 cm	60 cm
Clematis alpina 'Pink Flamingo'	Clematis	Apr–May	sun	well-drained	1.8 m	spreading
Clematis armandii 'Apple Blossom'	Clematis	Mar–Apr	sun	well-drained	5 m	spreading
Myosotis alpestris 'Rosylva'	Forget-me-not	Apr–May	sun/partial shade	well-drained/moist	15 cm	15 cm
Fritillaria meleagris p.32	Snake's head fritillary	Apr–May	sun	well-drained	20 cm	20 cm
Fritillaria michailovskyi	Fritillary	Apr–May	sun/partial shade	well-drained	20 cm	10 cm
Hyacinthus orientalis 'Woodstock'	Hyacinth	Apr–May	sun	well-drained	20 cm	10 cm
Lathyrus vernus	Perennial pea	Apr–May	sun	well-drained	30 cm	30 cm
Cardamine pratensis 'Flore Pleno'	Cuckoo flower	Apr–May	sun/partial shade	wet	25 cm	25 cm
Primula denticulata	Drumstick primula	Apr–May	sun	moist	30 cm	30 cm
Primula vulgaris 'Lilacina Plena'	Primrose	Apr–May	sun/partial shade	well-drained/moist	15 cm	15 cm
Pulsatilla vulgaris p.31	Pasque flower	Apr–May	sun	well-drained	30 cm	30 cm
Tulipa saxatilis (Bakeri Group) 'Lilac Wonder'	Tulip	Apr–May	sun	well-drained	15 cm	15 cm
Anthriscus sylvestris	Cow parsley	Apr–May	partial shade	well-drained	1 m	30 cm
Clematis alpina subsp. sibirica	Clematis	Apr–May	sun	well-drained	1.8 m	spreading
Clematis armandii p.30	Clematis	Mar–Apr	sun	well-drained	5 m	spreading
Clematis armandii 'Snowdrift'	Clematis	Mar–Apr	sun	well-drained	5 m	spreading
Dicentra formosa 'Aurora'	Bleeding heart	Apr–May	partial shade	moist	30 cm	25 cm
Dodecatheon meadia f. album	Shooting stars	Apr–May	shade	moist	30 cm	20 cm
Erythronium californicum 'White Beauty' p.26	Dog's tooth violet	Apr–May	partial shade	moist	20 cm	15 cm
Fritillaria meleagris subvar. alba	Snake's head fritillary	Apr–May	sun	moist	20 cm	5 cm
Galium odoratum	Sweet woodruff	Apr–May	partial shade	moist	20 cm	spreading
Hyacinthus orientalis 'Carnegie'	Hyacinth	Apr–May	sun	well-drained	20 cm	10 cm
Lamium maculatum 'White Nancy'	Dead nettle	Apr–Jul	shade	moist	30 cm	60 cm
Leucojum aestivum 'Gravetye Giant'	Summer snowflake	Apr–May	partial shade	moist	60 cm	20 cm
Myosotis alpestris 'Snowball'	Forget-me-not	Apr–May	sun/partial shade	well-drained/moist	15 cm	15 cm
Narcissus 'Cheerfulness'	Daffodil	Apr–May	sun	well-drained	40 cm	15 cm
Narcissus 'Ice Follies'	Daffodil	Apr–May	sun	well-drained	40 cm	15 cm
Narcissus 'Mount Hood'	Daffodil	Apr–May	sun	well-drained	45 cm	15 cm
Narcissus 'Thalia' p.27	Daffodil	Apr–May	sun	well-drained	35 cm	8 cm
Trillium grandiflorum p.25	Wake robin	Apr–Jun	shade	well-drained/moist	30 cm	30 cm
Primula auricula	Auricula	Apr–Jun	sun	well-drained	25 cm	15 cm
Viola tricolor 'Johnny Jump Up'	Heartsease	Apr–July	sun/partial shade	well-drained	15 cm	15 cm

spring: may

latin name	common name	flowering	sun/shade	moisture	height	spread
Aquilegia vulgaris 'Ruby Port'	Columbine	May–Jun	sun	well-drained	75 cm	45 cm

	Plant	Common name	Flowering	Light	Soil	Height	Spread
	Dodecatheon pulchellum 'Red Wings'	Shooting stars	May–Jun	shade	moist	30 cm	15 cm
	Geum 'Mrs J. Bradshaw'	Avens	May–Jul	sun	well-drained	50 cm	30 cm
	Paeonia officinalis 'Rubra Plena'	Peony	May–Jun	sun	well-drained/moist	75 cm	75 cm
	Papaver commutatum 'Ladybird'	Poppy	May–July	sun	well-drained/dry	45 cm	20 cm
	Primula japonica 'Miller's Crimson'	Candelabra primula	May–Jul	sun/partial shade	moist	60 cm	45 cm
	Primula pulverulenta	Candelabra primula	May–Jul	sun/partial shade	moist	60 cm	30 cm
	Anthemis sancti-johannis	Chamomile	May–Aug	sun	well-drained	45 cm	45 cm
	Calceolaria 'Sunset'	Lady's slipper	Jun–Oct	sun	well-drained	20 cm	10 cm
	Erysimum wheeleri	Wallflower	May–Oct	sun	well-drained	60 cm	45 cm
	Geum coccineum p.45	Avens	May–Jul	sun	well-drained	30 cm	30 cm
	Meconopsis cambrica 'Frances Perry'	Welsh poppy	May–Jun	sun	well-drained	30 cm	15 cm
	Erysimum 'Bredon'	Perennial wallflower	May–Oct	sun	well-drained	40 cm	50 cm
	Erysimum cheiri 'Harpur Crewe'	Perennial wallflower	May–Oct	sun	well-drained	75 cm	60 cm
	Euphorbia cyparissias	Cypress spurge	May–Jul	sun	dry	30 cm	30 cm
	Euphorbia × martinii	Spurge	May–Jul	sun	well-drained	60 cm	50 cm
	Geum 'Lady Stratheden'	Avens	May–Jul	sun	well-drained	50 cm	30 cm
	Meconopsis cambrica	Welsh poppy	May–Jul	sun	well-drained	45 cm	15 cm
	Primula veris	Cowslip	May–Jun	sun/partial shade	well-drained/moist	25 cm	15 cm
	Ranunculus acris 'Flore Pleno'	Bachelor's buttons	May–Jul	sun	moist	60 cm	45 cm
	Rosa banksiae 'Lutea' p.37	Banksian rose	May–Jun	sun/shelter	moist/well-fed	10 m	climbing
	Trollius × cultorum 'Goldquelle'	Globe flower	May–Jul	sun	moist/wet	60 cm	45 cm
	Tulipa 'West Point'	Tulip	Apr–May	sun	well-drained	50 cm	15 cm
	Aquilegia 'Yellow Star'	Columbine	May–Jun	sun	well-drained	75 cm	45 cm
	Camassia leichtlinii	Quamash	May–Jun	sun/partial shade	well-drained	60 cm	30 cm
	Digitalis lutea	Foxglove	May–Sept	partial shade	well-drained	60 cm	30 cm
	Disporum sessile 'Variegatum'	Fairy bells	May–Jun	partial shade	moist	30 cm	30 cm
	Geum rivale 'Leonard's Variety'	Water avens	May–Jul	sun	well-drained	30 cm	30 cm
	Paeonia mlokosewitschii p.46	Peony	May–Jun	sun	well-drained/moist	75 cm	75 cm
	Clematis 'Wada's Primrose'	Clematis	May–Jun	sun	well-drained	2.4 m	spreading
	Angelica archangelica	Angelica	May–Aug	sun/partial shade	moist	1.2 m	60 cm
	Aquilegia viridiflora	Columbine	May–Jun	sun	well-drained	30 cm	15 cm
	Smyrnium perfoliatum	Alexanders	May–Jul	partial shade	well-drained/moist	60 cm	60 cm
	Tulipa 'Spring Green'	Tulip	Apr–May	sun	well-drained	50 cm	15 cm
	Aquilegia caerulea	Columbine	May–Jun	sun	well-drained	60 cm	25 cm
	Camassia cusickii	Quamash	May–Jun	sun/partial shade	well-drained	60 cm	30 cm
	Meconopsis betonicifolia	Himalayan poppy	May–Jul	partial shade	moist/acid	90 cm	45 cm
	Nigella damascena 'Miss Jekyll' p.36	Love-in-a-mist	May–Jul	sun	well-drained	45 cm	15 cm
	Polemonium caeruleum	Jacob's ladder	May–Jul	sun	well-drained	60 cm	60 cm
	Veronica gentianoides	Speedwell	May–Jun	sun	well-drained/moist	45 cm	45 cm
	Dicentra spectabilis	Bleeding heart	May–Jul	partial shade	moist	60 cm	45 cm
	Gladiolus communis subsp. *byzantinus*	Gladiolus	May–Jun	sun	well-drained	60 cm	15 cm
	Osteospermum jucundum	Cape daisy	May–Oct	sun	well-drained	30 cm	30 cm
	Aquilegia vulgaris 'Nora Barlow' p.42	Columbine	May–Jun	sun	well-drained	75 cm	45 cm
	Armeria maritima	Thrift	May–Jul	sun		15 cm	25 cm
	Clematis 'Nelly Moser'	Clematis	May–Jun	shade	well-drained	2.4 m	spreading
	Dicentra formosa	Bleeding heart	May–Jul	partial shade	moist	60 cm	60 cm
	Digitalis purpurea	Foxglove	May–Jul	partial shade	well-drained	1.5 m	30 cm
	Rosa rubiginosa	Sweetbriar	May–Jul	sun	moist/well-fed	2.5 m	2.5 m
	Clematis montana 'Elizabeth' p.43	Clematis	May–Jun	sun	well-drained	6 m	spreading
	Clematis montana var. *rubens*	Clematis	May–Jun	sun	well-drained	6 m	spreading
	Papaver rhoeas 'Mother of Pearl'	Shirley poppy	May–July	sun	well-drained/dry	60 cm	15 cm
	Papaver somniferum 'Prolifers'	Hen and chickens	May–July	sun	well-drained/dry	75 cm	30 cm
	Tulipa 'Angélique'	Tulip	Apr–May	sun	well-drained	40 cm	15 cm
	Allium hollandicum 'Purple Sensation'	Ornamental onion	May–Jun	sun	well-drained	75 cm	25 cm
	Aquilegia vulgaris 'William Guinness'	Columbine	May–Jul	sun	well-drained	75 cm	45 cm
	Clematis 'Mrs N. Thompson'	Clematis	May–Aug	sun	well-drained	1.8 m	spreading
	Geranium phaeum 'Samobor' p.44	Cranesbill	May–Jul	partial shade	well-drained/dry	60 cm	60 cm
	Lunaria annua	Honesty	May–Jul	sun/partial shade	well-drained/moist	75 cm	30 cm
	Papaver somniferum 'Peony Black' p.41	Opium poppy	May–Jun	sun	well-drained/dry	90 cm	30 cm
	Tulipa 'Queen of Night' p.47	Tulip	Apr–May	sun	well-drained	60 cm	15 cm
	Clematis 'Mrs Cholmondeley'	Clematis	May–Sept	sun	well-drained	3 m	spreading
	Clematis 'Vyvyan Pennell'	Clematis	May–Jun	sun	well-drained	2.4 m	spreading
	Erysimum 'Bowles' Mauve p.40	Perennial wallflower	May–Oct	sun	well-drained	75 cm	60 cm
	Hesperis matronalis	Sweet rocket	May–Jul	sun	well-drained	90 cm	30 cm
	Phlox divaricata subsp. *laphamii* 'Chattahoochee'	Phlox	May–Jul	sun/partial shade	well-drained/moist	25 cm	25 cm
	Thalictrum aquilegiifolium 'Thundercloud'	Meadow rue	May–Jun	sun/partial shade	well-drained/moist	1 m	30 cm
	Tulipa 'Ballade'	Tulip	Apr–May	sun	well-drained	50 cm	15 cm
	Stachys byzantina	Lamb's ears	May–Oct	sun	dry	30 cm	60 cm
	Anthemis punctata subsp. *cupaniana*	Chamomile	May–Aug	sun	well-drained	35 cm	75 cm
	Aquilegia vulgaris 'Munstead White'	Columbine	May–Jul	sun	well-drained	75 cm	45 cm
	Armeria maritima 'Alba'	Thrift	May–Jul	sun	well-drained	15 cm	25 cm
	Asphodelus albus	Asphodel	May–Jun	sun	well-drained	90 cm	30 cm
	Clematis 'Belle of Woking'	Clematis	May–Jun	sun	well-drained	1.8 m	spreading
	Clematis montana	Clematis	May–Jun	sun	well-drained	6 m	spreading
	Convallaria majalis p.38	Lily-of-the-valley	May–Jun	partial shade	moist	20 cm	20 cm
	Convallaria majalis 'Fortin's Giant'	Lily-of-the-valley	May–Jun	partial shade	moist	25 cm	20 cm
	Convallaria majalis 'Variegata'	Lily-of-the-valley	May–Jun	partial shade	moist	20 cm	20 cm
	Dicentra spectabilis 'Alba' p.39	Bleeding heart	May–Jul	partial shade	moist	60 cm	45 cm
	Digitalis purpurea f. *albiflora*	Foxglove	May–Jul	partial shade	well-drained	1.5 m	30 cm
	Erigeron karvinskianus	Fleabane	May–Sept	sun	well-drained	20 cm	20 cm
	Gladiolus × colvillei 'The Bride'	Gladiolus	May–Jun	sun	well-drained	60 cm	20 cm
	Libertia grandiflora	Libertia	May–Jun	sun	well-drained	45 cm	25 cm
	Lunaria annua var. *albiflora*	Honesty	May–Jul	sun/partial shade	well-drained/moist	75 cm	30 cm
	Narcissus poeticus var. *recurvus*	Pheasant's eye narcissus	May–Jun	sun	well-drained	35 cm	10 cm
	Nigella 'Miss Jekyll Alba'	Love-in-a-mist	Jun–Sept	sun	well-drained	45 cm	15 cm
	Osteospermum 'White Pim'	Cape daisy	May–Oct	sun	well-drained	30 cm	30 cm
	Polemonium 'Dawn Flight'	Jacob's ladder	May–Jul	sun	well-drained	60 cm	60 cm

latin name	common name	flowering	sun/shade	moisture	height	spread
Polygonatum × hybridum	Solomon's seal	May–Jul	partial shade	moist	90 cm	60 cm
Smilacina racemosa	False spikenard	May–Jun	shade	moist	75 cm	45 cm
Tiarella cordifolia	Foam flower	Apr–May	sun	well-drained	20 cm	15 cm
Anemone De Caen Group	Anemone	May–Jun	sun	well-drained	25 cm	10 cm
Viola tricolor	Heartsease	May–Sept	sun/partial shade	well-drained	15 cm	15 cm

summer: june

latin name	common name	flowering	sun/shade	moisture	height	spread
Antirrhinum majus 'Black Prince'	Snapdragon	Jun–Sep	sun	well-drained	45 cm	25 cm
Astrantia major 'Hadspen Blood' p.55	Masterwort	Jun–Oct	sun	well-drained	60 cm	45 cm
Astrantia major 'Lars'	Masterwort	Jun–Oct	partial shade	well-drained	60 cm	45 cm
Atriplex hortensis var. rubra	Red orach	Jun–Oct	sun	well-drained	1.2 m	45 cm
Clematis 'Rouge Cardinal'	Clematis	Jun–Sep	sun	well-drained	1.8 m	spreading
Dianthus barbatus 'Sooty'	Sweet william	Jun–Aug	sun	well-drained	30 cm	30 cm
Lathyrus odoratus 'Midnight'	Sweet pea	Jun–Sep	sun	well-drained	1.8 m	climbing
Lobularia maritima 'Trailing Rosy Red'	Alyssum	Jun–Oct	sun	well-drained	10 cm	50 cm
Pelargonium 'Lord Bute'	Regal pelargonium	Jun–Sep	sun	well-drained	60 cm	45 cm
Pelargonium 'Tomcat'	Ivy-leaved pelargonium	Jun–Oct	sun	well-drained	30 cm	trailing
Petunia 'Primetime Burgundy'	Multiflora petunia	Jun–Oct	sun	well-drained	30 cm	30 cm
Rosa 'Louis XIV'	Rose	Jun–Sep	sun	moist/well-fed	60 cm	60 cm
Rosa 'William Shakespeare 2000'	Rose	Jun–Sep	sun	moist/well-fed	1.2 m	1 m
Verbena × hybrida 'Quartz Burgundy'	Verbena	Jun–Oct	sun	well-drained	25 cm	25 cm
Centranthus ruber	Red valerian	Jun–Sep	sun	dry	60 cm	45 cm
Clematis 'Dr Ruppel'	Clematis	Jun–Sep	sun	well-drained	2.4 m	spreading
Clematis 'Niobe' p.53	Clematis	Jun–Sep	sun	well-drained	2.4 m	spreading
Delphinium nudicaule	Delphinium	Jun–Aug	sun	well-drained/moist	60 cm	30 cm
Dianthus 'Sops in Wine' p.51	Pink	Jun–Aug	sun	well-drained	25 cm	25 cm
Echium russicum	Russian bugloss	Jun–Aug	sun/shelter	well-drained	60 cm	45 cm
Eschscholzia californica 'Inferno'	California poppy	Jun–Oct	sun	well-drained	30 cm	15 cm
Gaillardia 'Burgunder'	Blanket flower	Jun–Oct	sun	well-drained	60 cm	30 cm
Gaillardia pulchella 'Red Plume'	Blanket flower	Jun–Oct	sun	well-drained	25 cm	25 cm
Impatiens walleriana 'Super Elfin Velvet Red'	Busy lizzie	Jun–Oct	partial shade/sun	well-drained	25 cm	20 cm
Iris 'Holden Clough'	Iris	Jun–Jul	sun	well-drained	90 cm	30 cm
Linum grandiflorum 'Rubrum'	Flax	Jun–Aug	sun	well-drained	45 cm	20 cm
Lobelia erinus 'Cascade Red'	Lobelia	Jun–Oct	sun	well-drained	15 cm	trailing
Lychnis chalcedonica	Maltese cross	Jun–Aug	sun	moist	1 m	30 cm
Lychnis × arkwrightii 'Vesuvius'	Campion	Jun–Aug	sun	well-drained	30 cm	25 cm
Nemesia strumosa 'Fire King'	Nemesia	Jun–Sep	sun	well-drained	20 cm	15 cm
Papaver orientale 'Beauty of Livermere'	Oriental poppy	May–Jun	sun	well-drained/dry	1 m	60 cm
Pelargonium 'Ardens'	Species pelargonium	Jun–Oct	sun	well-drained	20 cm	20 cm
Pelargonium 'Conspicuous'	Regal pelargonium	Jun–Sep	sun	well-drained	45 cm	45 cm
Pelargonium 'Crampel's Crimson'	Zonal pelargonium	Jun–Oct	sun	well-drained	45 cm	45 cm
Pelargonium 'Jacko'	Ivy-leaved pelargonium	Jun–Oct	sun	well-drained	30 cm	trailing
Persicaria affinis 'Darjeeling Red'	Knotweed	Jun–Sep	sun	moist	25 cm	60 cm
Tagetes patula 'Durango Red'	French marigold	Jun–Sep	sun	well-drained	20 cm	10 cm
Tropaeolum majus 'Empress of India'	Nasturtium	Jun–Oct	sun	well-drained	30 cm	30 cm
Viola 'Arkwright Ruby'	Viola	Jun–Sep	sun/partial shade	well-drained	15 cm	15 cm
Arctotis hirsuta	African daisy	Jun–Oct	sun	well-drained	45 cm	20 cm
Calendula officinalis	Pot marigold	Jun–Sep	sun	well-drained	60 cm	15 cm
Digitalis ferruginea	Rusty foxglove	Jun–Aug	sun/partial shade	well-drained	1.2 m	30 cm
Eccremocarpus scaber	Chilean glory flower	Jun–Sep	sun	well-drained	1.8 m	spreading
Eremurus × isabellinus 'Cleopatra'	Foxtail lily	Jun–Jul	sun	well-drained	1.2 m	60 cm
Eremurus stenophyllus	Foxtail lily	Jun–Jul	sun	well-drained	1.2 m	60 cm
Hemerocallis 'Buzz Bomb'	Daylily	Jun–Aug	sun/partial shade	well-drained	90 cm	60 cm
Iris 'Kent Pride'	Bearded iris	Jun–Jul	sun	well-drained	90 cm	30 cm
Iris 'Tangerine Sky'	Bearded iris	Jun–Jul	sun	well-drained	1.2 m	60 cm
Oenothera versicolor 'Sunset Boulevard'	Evening primrose	Jun–Aug	sun	well-drained	60 cm	45 cm
Papaver nudicaule	Iceland poppy	Jun–Aug	sun	well-drained/dry	45 cm	25 cm
Pelargonium 'Dryden'	Zonal pelargonium	Jun–Oct	sun	well-drained	45 cm	45 cm
Pelargonium 'Mrs Pollock'	Zonal geranium	Jun–Oct	sun	well-drained	30 cm	30 cm
Antirrhinum majus 'Peaches and Cream'	Snapdragon	Jun–Sep	sun	well-drained	20 cm	15 cm
Calendula officinalis 'Pacific Apricot'	Pot marigold	Jun–Sep	sun	well-drained	70 cm	15 cm
Clarkia amoena 'Salmon Princess'	Godetia	Jun–Sep	sun	well-drained	30 cm	20 cm
Digitalis purpurea 'Sutton's Apricot'	Foxglove	Jun–Jul	partial shade	well-drained	1.5 m	30 cm
Eremurus × isabellinus Ruiter hybrids	Foxtail lily	Jun–Jul	sun	well-drained	1.5 m	60 cm
Eschscholzia californica 'Apricot Flambeau'	California poppy	Jun–Oct	sun	well-drained	25 cm	15 cm
Impatiens walleriana 'Tempo Peach Frost'	Busy lizzie	Jun–Oct	partial shade/sun	well-drained	25 cm	20 cm
Oenothera 'Apricot Delight'	Evening primrose	Jun–Aug	sun	well-drained	90 cm	45 cm
Scabiosa atropurpurea 'Salmon Queen'	Pincushion flower	Jun–Sep	sun	well-drained	90 cm	30 cm
Thunbergia alata	Black-eyed Susan	Jun–Sep	sun	well-drained/moist	3 m	climbing
Tropaeolum majus 'Peach Melba'	Nasturtium	Jun–Oct	sun	well-drained	25 cm	25 cm
Verbascum 'Helen Johnson'	Mullein	Jun–Aug	sun	well-drained	90 cm	30 cm
Verbena 'Peaches and Cream'	Verbena	Jun–Oct	sun	well-drained	20 cm	20 cm
Alchemilla erythropoda	Lady's mantle	Jun–Sep	sun/shade	any	30 cm	30 cm
Alchemilla mollis p.52	Lady's mantle	Jun–Aug	sun/shade	any	45 cm	45 cm
Antirrhinum braun-blanquetii	Snapdragon	Jun–Sep	sun	well-drained	30 cm	25 cm
Asphodeline lutea	Asphodel	Jun–Aug	sun	dry	1 m	30 cm
Coreopsis grandiflora	Tickseed	Jun–Aug	sun	well-drained	75 cm	40 cm
Eschscholzia californica p.61	California poppy	Jun–Oct	sun	well-drained	30 cm	15 cm
Gaillardia 'Indian Yellow'	Blanket flower	Jun–Oct	sun	well-drained	60 cm	30 cm
Gentiana lutea	Gentian	Jun–Aug	sun	moist	1.2 m	60 cm
Hemerocallis 'Corky'	Daylily	Jun–Sep	sun/partial shade	well-drained	45 cm	45 cm

Hemerocallis lilioasphodelus	Daylily	May–Jun	sun/partial shade	well-drained	75 cm	45 cm
Hemerocallis 'Stella de Oro'	Daylily	Jun–Oct	sun/partial shade	well-drained	50 cm	45 cm
Iris pseudacorus	Yellow flag	Jun–Jul	sun	moist	1 m	30 cm
Iris sibirica 'Dreaming Yellow'	Siberian iris	Jun–Jul	sun	moist	90 cm	30 cm
Limnanthes douglasii	Poached egg plant	Jun–Sep	sun	well-drained	15 cm	15 cm
Lupinus **'Chandelier'** p.62	Lupin	Jun–Jul	sun	well-drained	1 m	60 cm
Lysimachia ciliata 'Firecracker'	Loosestrife	Jun–Aug	sun/partial shade	moist	90 cm	60 cm
Mimulus 'Puck'	Monkey flower	Jun–Aug	sun	moist	15 cm	25 cm
Oenothera biennis	Evening primrose	Jun–Aug	sun	well-drained	90 cm	60 cm
Oenothera fruticosa Fireworks	Evening primrose	Jun–Aug	sun	well-drained	35 cm	30 cm
Primula florindae	Himalayan cowslip	Jun–Aug	sun/partial shade	moist	60 cm	30 cm
Rosa 'Graham Thomas'	Rose	Jun–Sep	sun	moist/well-fed	1.5 m	1.5 m
Roscoea cautleyoides	Roscoea	May–Jul	partial shade	moist	50 cm	10 cm
Stokesia laevis 'Mary Gregory'	Stokes's aster	Jun–Sep	sun	well-drained	45 cm	45 cm
Tagetes tenuifolia 'Lemon Gem'	French marigold	Jun–Sep	sun	well-drained	5 cm	10 cm
Cephalaria gigantea	Giant scabious	Jun–Sep	sun	well-drained	1.8 m	1.2 m
Digitalis grandiflora	Foxglove	Jun–Aug	partial shade	well-drained	60 cm	30 cm
Iris 'Star Shine'	Bearded iris	Jun–Jul	sun	well-drained	1.2 m	60 cm
Petunia 'Banana Milkshake'	Grandiflora petunia	Jun–Oct	sun	well-drained	30 cm	30 cm
Tropaeolum majus 'Moonlight'	Climbing nasturtium	Jun–Oct	sun	well-drained	1.8 m	climbing
Aconitum 'Ivorine'	Monkshood	Jun–Jul	partial shade	moist	50 cm	45 cm
Campanula takesimana	Bellflower	Jun–Aug	sun/partial shade	well-drained	75 cm	30 cm
Clematis florida 'Flore Pleno'	Clematis	Jun–Sep	sun	well-drained	1.8 m	spreading
Clematis 'Henryi'	Clematis	Jun–Sep	sun	well-drained	3 m	spreading
Clematis 'Miss Batemen'	Clematis	May–Jun	sun	well-drained	1.8 m	spreading
Delphinium 'Sungleam'	Delphinium	Jun–Jul	sun	well-drained/moist	1.5 m	60 cm
Eschscholzia californica 'Buttermilk'	California poppy	Jun–Oct	sun	well-drained	25 cm	15 cm
Lathyrus odoratus 'Cream Southbourne'	Sweet pea	Jun–Sep	sun	well-drained	1.8 m	climbing
Lupinus 'Noble Maiden'	Lupin	Jun–Jul	sun	well-drained	1 m	60 cm
Paeonia lactiflora 'Duchesse de Nemours'	Peony	May–Jun	sun	well-drained/moist	70 cm	70 cm
Rosa **'Buff Beauty'** p.56	Rose	Jun–Sep	sun/partial shade	moist/well-fed	1.5 m	1.5 m
Arisaema consanguineum	Arisaema	Jun–Jul	partial shade	moist	60 cm	30 cm
Codonopsis viridiflora	Codonopsis	Jun–Sep	sun/partial shade	well-drained	1.8 m	climbing
Reseda odorata	Mignonette	Jun–Sep	sun	well-drained	30 cm	25 cm
Anchusa azurea 'Loddon Royalist'	Anchusa	Jun–Jul	sun	well-drained	1.2 m	60 cm
Delphinium 'Black Knight'	Delphinium	Jun–Aug	sun	well-drained/moist	1.5 m	60 cm
Iris 'Deep Pacific'	Bearded iris	Jun–Jul	sun	well-drained	90 cm	30 cm
Iris sibirica	Siberian iris	Jun–Jul	sun	moist	90 cm	25 cm
Lobelia erinus 'Crystal Palace'	Lobelia	Jun–Oct	sun	well-drained	15 cm	15 cm
Lobelia erinus 'Sapphire'	Lobelia	Jun–Oct	sun	well-drained	15 cm	trailing
Adenophora bulleyana	Ladybells	Jun–Aug	sun	well-drained	60 cm	30 cm
Ageratum houstonianum 'Blue Danube'	Ageratum	Jun–Aug	sun	well-drained	15 cm	15 cm
Baptisia australis	Blue wild indigo	Jun–Aug	sun	well-drained	90 cm	60 cm
Borago officinalis	Borage	Jun–Aug	sun	well-drained	60 cm	45 cm
Campanula carpatica	Bellflower	Jun–Aug	sun/partial shade	well-drained	30 cm	30 cm
Campanula persicifolia	Bellflower	Jun–Aug	sun/partial shade	well-drained	70 cm	30 cm
Campanula portenschlagiana	Bellflower	Jun–Aug	sun	well-drained	15 cm	1 m
Centaurea cyanus 'Blue Diadem'	Cornflower	Jun–Aug	sun	well-drained	60 cm	15 cm
Centaurea montana	Perennial cornflower	Jun–Sep	sun	well-drained	50 cm	60 cm
Clematis 'General Sikorski'	Clematis	Jun–Aug	sun	well-drained	2.4 m	spreading
Clematis integrifolia	Herbaceous clematis	Jun–Sep	sun	well-drained	90 cm	spreading
Clematis × *durandii*	Herbaceous clematis	Jun–Sep	sun	well-drained	1.8 m	spreading
Convolvulus sabatius	Dwarf morning glory	Jun–Sep	sun	well-drained	15 cm	trailing
Delphinium Belladonna Group 'Blue Bees'	Delphinium	Jun–July	sun	well-drained/moist	1.2 m	60 cm
Delphinium grandiflorum **'Blue Butterfly'** p.50	Delphinium	Jun–Aug	sun	well-drained/moist	45 cm	30 cm
Echium pininana	Pride of Tenerife	Jun–Aug	sun/shelter	well-drained	4 m	1 m
Echium vulgare 'Blue Bedder'	Viper's bugloss	Jun–Aug	sun	well-drained	45 cm	30 cm
Eryngium alpinum	Sea holly	Jun–Aug	sun	well-drained	90 cm	45 cm
Eryngium bourgatii 'Oxford Blue'	Sea holly	Jun–Sep	sun	well-drained	60 cm	30 cm
Eryngium planum	Sea holly	Jun–Sep	sun	well-drained	1.5 m	60 cm
Eryngium × *oliverianum*	Sea holly	Jun–Aug	sun	well-drained	90 cm	45 cm
Felicia bergeriana	Kingfisher daisy	Jun–Sep	sun	well-drained	25 cm	25 cm
Geranium 'Brookside'	Cranesbill	Jun–Aug	sun	well-drained	45 cm	45 cm
Geranium himalayense	Cranesbill	Jun–Sep	sun	well-drained	30 cm	45 cm
Geranium himalayense 'Plenum'	Cranesbill	Jun–Aug	sun	well-drained	30 cm	25 cm
Geranium ibericum	Cranesbill	Jun–Jul	sun	well-drained	60 cm	60 cm
Geranium 'Johnson's Blue'	Cranesbill	Jun–Sep	sun	well-drained	45 cm	45 cm
Geranium **'Rozanne'** p.54	Cranesbill	Jun–Oct	sun	well-drained	60 cm	90 cm
Hyssopus officinalis	Hyssop	Jun–Aug	sun	well-drained	50 cm	30 cm
Iris ensata	Japanese iris	Jun–Jul	sun	moist	90 cm	30 cm
Limonium sinuatum 'Azure'	Statice	Jun–Sep	sun	well-drained	60 cm	10 cm
Lupinus 'The Governor'	Lupin	Jun–Jul	sun	well-drained	1 m	60 cm
Malva sylvestris 'Primley Blue'	Mallow	Jun–Sep	sun	well-drained	90 cm	30 cm
Meconopsis grandis	Himalayan poppy	Jun–Jul	partial shade	moist	1 m	25 cm
Nemesia strumosa 'KLM'	Nemesia	Jun–Sep	sun	well-drained	20 cm	15 cm
Nepeta 'Six Hills Giant'	Catmint	Jun–Sep	sun	well-drained	90 cm	60 cm
Nepeta × *faassenii*	Catmint	Jun–Sep	sun	well-drained	45 cm	45 cm
Omphalodes cappadocica 'Starry Eyes'	Navelwort	Jun–Jul	partial shade	moist	25 cm	25 cm
Petunia 'Blue Daddy'	Grandiflora petunia	Jun–Oct	sun	well-drained	30 cm	30 cm
Petunia 'Dreams Midnight Blue'	Grandiflora petunia	Jun–Oct	sun	well-drained	30 cm	30 cm
Phacelia campanularia	Californian bluebell	Jun–Sep	sun	well-drained	25 cm	15 cm
Stokesia laevis	Stokes's aster	Jun–Sep	sun	well-drained	30 cm	30 cm
Viola cornuta p.58	Viola	May–Aug	sun/partial shade	well-drained	15 cm	30 cm
Viola 'Maggie Mott'	Viola	May–Aug	sun/partial shade	well-drained	15 cm	15 cm
Clematis 'Lasurstern'	Clematis	Jun–Aug	sun	well-drained	2.4 m	spreading
Clematis 'William Kennett'	Clematis	Jun–Sep	sun	well-drained	3 m	spreading
Consolida 'Frosted Skies'	Larkspur	Jun–Sep	sun	well-drained	90 cm	25 cm

Iris 'Jane Phillips'	Bearded iris	Jun–Jul	sun	well-drained	90 cm	30 cm
Iris pallida 'Argentea Variegata'	Bearded iris	Jun–Jul	sun	well-drained	60 cm	30 cm
Iris sibirica 'Mrs Rowe'	Siberian iris	Jun–Jul	sun	moist	90 cm	30 cm
Linum narbonense 'Heavenly Blue'	Flax	Jun–Aug	sun	well-drained	45 cm	20 cm
Linum perenne	Flax	Jun–Aug	sun	well-drained	60 cm	30 cm
Lobelia erinus 'Cambridge Blue'	Lobelia	Jun–Oct	sun	well-drained	15 cm	15 cm
Lobelia erinus 'Regatta Marine'	Lobelia	Jun–Oct	sun	well-drained	15 cm	trailing
Meconopsis 'Branklyn'	Himalayan poppy	Jun–Jul	partial shade	moist/acid	90 cm	35 cm
Nemophila menziesii 'Blue'	Baby blue eyes	Jun–Aug	sun	well-drained/moist	15 cm	15 cm
Scabiosa caucasica 'Clive Greaves'	Scabious	Jun–Sep	sun	well-drained	60 cm	45 cm
Clematis 'Hagley Hybrid'	Clematis	Jun–Sep	sun	well-drained	1.8 m	spreading
Coreopsis rosea 'American Dream'	Pink tickseed	May–Aug	sun	well-drained	40 cm	20 cm
Eschscholzia californica 'Purple Cap'	California poppy	Jun–Oct	sun	well-drained	30 cm	15 cm
Filipendula rubra 'Venusta'	Queen of the prairies	Jun–Aug	sun	moist	1.8 m	1.2 m
Geranium macrorrhizum	Cranesbill	Jun–Jul	shade	dry	25 cm	60 cm
Geranium maderense	Cranesbill	Jun–Jul	sun/sheltered	well-drained	1 m	90 cm
Incarvillea delavayi	Incarvillea	Jun–July	sun	well-drained	40 cm	30 cm
Incarvillea mairei	Incarvillea	Jun–July	sun	well-drained	30 cm	30 cm
Lathyrus grandiflorus	Perennial pea	Jun–Sep	sun	well-drained	2 m	climbing
Lathyrus odoratus 'Zorija Rose'	Sweet pea	Jun–Sep	sun	well-drained	1.8 m	climbing
Lilium martagon	Turkscap lily	Jun–Jul	partial shade/sun	well-drained	1.2 m	15 cm
Lupinus 'My Castle'	Lupin	Jun–Jul	sun	well-drained	1 m	60 cm
Schizanthus hookeri	Poor man's orchid	Jun–Oct	sun	well-drained/moist	45 cm	30 cm
Verbena 'Raspberry Crush'	Verbena	Jun–Oct	sun	well-drained	30 cm	30 cm
Ageratum houstonianum 'Pinky Improved'	Ageratum	Jun–Aug	sun	well-drained	15 cm	15 cm
Agrostemma githago	Corncockle	Jun–Aug	sun	well-drained	90 cm	20 cm
Allium schubertii	Ornamental onion	Jun–Jul	sun	well-drained	60 cm	25 cm
Astrantia major 'Sunningdale Variegated'	Masterwort	Jun–Oct	partial shade	well-drained	60 cm	45 cm
Calamintha grandiflora	Calamint	Jun–Sep	sun	well-drained	45 cm	30 cm
Centaurea dealbata	Knapweed	Jun–Sep	sun	well-drained	60 cm	45 cm
Clarkia amoena 'Thoroughly Modern Millie'	Godetia	Jun–Sep	sun	well-drained	45 cm	20 cm
Clematis 'Asao'	Clematis	Jun–Sep	sun	well-drained	1.8 m	spreading
Clematis 'Bees' Jubilee'	Clematis	Jun–Sep	sun	well-drained	1.8 m	spreading
Dianthus 'Pike's Pink'	Pink	Jun–Aug	sun	well-drained	25 cm	25 cm
Digitalis × mertonensis p.59	Foxglove	Jun–Aug	partial shade	well-drained	60 cm	30 cm
Eschscholzia californica 'Rose Chiffon'	California poppy	Jun–Oct	sun	well-drained	25 cm	15 cm
Geranium cinereum 'Ballerina'	Cranesbill	Jun–Sep	sun	well-drained	15 cm	15 cm
Geranium × oxonianum 'Claridge Druce'	Cranesbill	Jun–Sep	sun	well-drained	60 cm	60 cm
Geranium × oxonianum 'Wargrave Pink'	Cranesbill	Jun–Sep	sun	well-drained	60 cm	60 cm
Hemerocallis 'Catherine Woodbery'	Daylily	Jun–Aug	sun/partial shade	well-drained	90 cm	60 cm
Impatiens walleriana 'Accent Midnight Rose'	Busy lizzie	Jun–Oct	partial shade/sun	well-drained	35 cm	25 cm
Lathyrus latifolius 'Pink Pearl'	Perennial pea	Jun–Aug	sun	well-drained	1.5 m	climbing
Linaria purpurea 'Canon Went'	Toadflax	Jun–Aug	sun	well-drained/dry	90 cm	45 cm
Lupinus 'The Chatelaine'	Lupin	Jun–Jul	sun	well-drained	1 m	60 cm
Matthiola incana 'Apple Blossom'	Stock	Jun–Aug	sun	well-drained	30 cm	25 cm
Oenothera speciosa 'Pink Petticoats'	Pinkladies	Jun–Sep	sun	well-drained	30 cm	30 cm
Oenothera speciosa 'Siskiyou'	Pinkladies	Jun–Aug	sun	well-drained	30 cm	30 cm
Paeonia lactiflora 'Bowl of Beauty'	Peony	May–Jun	sun	well-drained/moist	90 cm	90 cm
Paeonia lactiflora 'Sarah Bernhardt'	Peony	May–Jun	sun	well-drained/moist	1 m	1 m
Papaver orientale 'Mrs Perry'	Oriental poppy	May–Jun	sun	well-drained/dry	75 cm	60 cm
Papaver orientale 'Patty's Plum' p.63	Oriental poppy	May–Jun	sun	well-drained/dry	75 cm	60 cm
Papaver orientale 'Princess Alexandra'	Oriental poppy	May–Jun	sun	well-drained/dry	75 cm	60 cm
Pelargonium 'Harewood Slam'	Regal pelargonium	Jun–Sep	sun	well-drained	45 cm	45 cm
Pelargonium 'Maverick Star'	Zonal geranium	Jun–Oct	sun	well-drained	30 cm	30 cm
Persicaria bistorta 'Superba'	Bistort	May–Jul	sun	moist	80 cm	60 cm
Petunia 'Pink Wave'	Trailing petunia	Jun–Oct	sun	well-drained	15 cm	trailing
Sidalcea 'Loveliness'	False mallow	Jun–Aug	sun/partial shade	well-drained	75 cm	45 cm
Verbascum 'Megan's Mauve'	Mullein	Jun–Aug	sun	well-drained	90 cm	30 cm
Campanula lactiflora 'Loddon Anna'	Bellflower	Jun–Aug	sun/partial shade	well-drained	1.8 m	60 cm
Delphinium Astolat Group	Delphinium	Jun–Aug	sun	well-drained/moist	1.5 m	60 cm
Dianthus 'Doris'	Pink	Jun–Aug	sun	well-drained	30 cm	30 cm
Dictamnus albus var. purpureus	Burning bush	Jun–Aug	sun	well-drained	80 cm	60 cm
Francoa ramosa	Bridal wreath	Jun–Aug	partial shade	well-drained	75 cm	30 cm
Francoa sonchifolia	Bridal wreath	Jun–Aug	partial shade	well-drained	60 cm	30 cm
Gypsophila Rosy Veil ('Rosenschleier')	Baby's breath	Jun–Aug	sun	well-drained	30 cm	45 cm
Matthiola incana 'Cinderella Antique Pink'	Stock	Jun–Aug	sun	well-drained	25 cm	15 cm
Petunia 'Dream Appleblossom'	Grandiflora petunia	Jun–Oct	sun	well-drained	30 cm	30 cm
Allium giganteum	Ornamental onion	Jun–Jul	sun	well-drained	1.3 m	25 cm
Astrantia major 'Primadonna'	Masterwort	Jun–Oct	sun	well-drained	60 cm	45 cm
Campanula glomerata 'Superba'	Bellflower	Jun–Aug	sun/partial shade	well-drained	60 cm	30 cm
Campanula lactiflora 'Prichard's Variety' p.57	Bellflower	Jun–Aug	sun/partial shade	well-drained	1.5 m	60 cm
Centaurea cyanus 'Black Ball'	Cornflower	Jun–Aug	sun	well-drained	60 cm	15 cm
Clematis 'Jackmanii Superba'	Clematis	Jun–Sep	sun	well-drained	3 m	spreading
Clematis 'The President'	Clematis	Jun–Sep	sun	well-drained	2.4 m	spreading
Cuphea × purpurea	Cuphea	Jun–Oct	sun	well-drained	60 cm	45 cm
Erigeron 'Dunkelste Alle'	Fleabane	Jun–Aug	sun	well-drained	60 cm	45 cm
Hemerocallis 'Root Beer'	Daylily	Jun–Aug	sun/partial shade	well-drained	100 cm	60 cm
Iris 'Black Swan' p.64	Bearded iris	Jun–Jul	sun	well-drained	90 cm	30 cm
Iris chrysographes 'Black Knight'	Iris	Jun–Jul	sun	moist	70 cm	30 cm
Nemophila menziesii var. discoidalis	Baby blue eyes	Jun–Aug	sun	well-drained/moist	15 cm	15 cm
Petunia 'Purple Wave'	Trailing petunia	Jun–Oct	sun	well-drained	15 cm	trailing
Salvia × sylvestris 'Mainacht'	Sage	May–Aug	sun	well-drained	45 cm	30 cm
Veronica 'Romiley Purple'	Speedwell	Jun–Aug	sun	well-drained	45 cm	30 cm
Viola 'Bowles' Black'	Viola	May–Aug	sun/partial shade	well-drained	15 cm	15 cm
Adenophora 'Amethyst'	Ladybells	Jun–Aug	sun	well-drained	90 cm	45 cm
Allium cristophii p.65	Ornamental onion	Jun–Jul	sun	well-drained	45 cm	25 cm
Allium 'Globemaster'	Ornamental onion	Jun–Jul	sun	well-drained	1.2 m	25 cm

	Plant	Common name	Flowering	Light	Soil	Height	Spread
	Campanula poscharskyana	Bellflower	Jun–Aug	sun	well-drained	15 cm	60 cm
	Campanula pyramidalis	Chimney bellflower	Jun–Aug	sun/partial shade	well-drained	1.2 m	60 cm
	Centaurea cyanus 'Mauve Queen'	Cornflower	Jun–Aug	sun	well-drained	60 cm	15 cm
	Clarkia bottae 'Amethyst Glow'	Godetia	Jun–Sep	sun	well-drained	30 cm	20 cm
	Clarkia tenella 'Lady in Blue'	Godetia	Jun–Sep	sun	well-drained	30 cm	20 cm
	Clematis 'Barbara Jackman'	Clematis	Jun–Sep	sun	well-drained	2.4 m	spreading
	Clematis 'Elsa Späth'	Clematis	Jun–Sep	sun	well-drained	1.8 m	spreading
	Consolida 'Earl Grey'	Larkspur	Jun–Sep	sun	well-drained	90 cm	25 cm
	Delphinium 'Fanfare'	Delphinium	Jun–Aug	sun	well-drained/moist	1.5 m	60 cm
	Erigeron 'Quakeress'	Fleabane	Jun–Aug	sun	well-drained	60 cm	45 cm
	Galega officinalis	Goat's rue	Jun–Aug	sun	well-drained	1.5 m	90 cm
	Geranium clarkei 'Kashmir Purple'	Cranesbill	Jun–Aug	sun	well-drained	30 cm	45 cm
	Geranium pratense 'Mrs Kendall Clark'	Cranesbill	Jun–Jul	sun	well-drained	60 cm	60 cm
	Geranium × magnificum	Cranesbill	Jun–Jul	sun	well-drained	60 cm	60 cm
	Hemerocallis 'Amazon Amethyst'	Daylily	Jun–Aug	sun/partial shade	well-drained	90 cm	60 cm
	Impatiens walleriana 'Blue Pearl'	Busy lizzie	Jun–Oct	partial shade/sun	well-drained	25 cm	20 cm
	Lobularia maritima 'Royal Carpet'	Alyssum	Jun–Oct	sun	well-drained	8 cm	25 cm
	Nemesia caerulea 'Coconut Ice'	Nemesia	Jun–Sep	sun	well-drained	30 cm	15 cm
	Petunia 'Plum Crystals'	Multiflora petunia	Jun–Oct	sun	well-drained	30 cm	30 cm
	Phacelia dubia 'Lavender Lass'	Scorpion weed	Jun–Sep	sun	well-drained	30 cm	25 cm
	Primula vialii	Primula	Jun–Aug	sun/partial shade	well-drained/moist	30 cm	20 cm
	Prunella grandiflora 'Loveliness'	Self-heal	Jun–Aug	sun/partial shade	moist	15 cm	45 cm
	Rosa 'Veilchenblau'	Rambler rose	Jun–Jul	sun/partial shade	moist/well-fed	4.5 m	climbing
	Scabiosa stellata	Drumstick scabious	Jun–Sep	sun	well-drained	45 cm	25 cm
	Schizanthus grahamii	Poor man's orchid	Jun–Oct	sun	well-drained/moist	45 cm	30 cm
	Stachys macrantha 'Superba'	Lamb's ears	Jun–Aug	sun	well-drained	30 cm	30 cm
	Verbena 'Imagination'	Verbena	Jun–Oct	sun	well-drained	30 cm	30 cm
	Verbena 'La France'	Verbena	Jun–Oct	sun	well-drained	60 cm	30 cm
	Salvia argentea	Salvia	Jun–Jul	sun	well-drained/dry	90 cm	45 cm
	Senecio cineraria 'Cirrus'	Senecio	Jun–Oct	sun	well-drained	30 cm	30 cm
	Senecio cineraria 'Silver Dust'	Senecio	Jun–Oct	sun	well-drained	30 cm	30 cm
	Ageratum houstonianum 'Summer Snow'	Ageratum	Jun–Aug	sun	well-drained	15 cm	15 cm
	Agrostemma githago 'Ocean Pearl'	Corncockle	Jun–Aug	sun	well-drained	90 cm	20 cm
	Antirrhinum majus 'Royal Bride'	Snapdragon	Jun–Sep	sun	well-drained	60 cm	30 cm
	Arisaema candidissimum	Arisaema	Jun–Aug	partial shade	moist	30 cm	45 cm
	Aruncus dioicus	Goat's beard	Jun–Jul	partial shade	moist	1.2 m	90 cm
	Aruncus dioicus 'Kneiffii'	Goat's beard	Jun–Jul	partial shade	moist	90 cm	45 cm
	Astrantia major 'Shaggy'	Masterwort	Jun–Oct	partial shade	well-drained	90 cm	45 cm
	Calceolaria alba	Lady's slipper	Jun–Sep	sun	well-drained	60 cm	45 cm
	Campanula persicifolia 'Alba'	Bellflower	Jun–Aug	sun/partial shade	well-drained	70 cm	30 cm
	Centranthus ruber 'Albus'	Valerian	Jun–Sep	sun	dry	60 cm	45 cm
	Clematis 'Edith'	Clematis	Jun–Sep	sun	well-drained	3 m	spreading
	Clematis florida 'Sieboldii'	Clematis	Jun–Sep	sun	well-drained	1.8 m	spreading
	Clematis 'Gillian Blades'	Clematis	Jun–Sep	sun	well-drained	1.8 m	spreading
	Clematis 'Marie Boisselot'	Clematis	Jun–Sep	sun	well-drained	3 m	spreading
	Clematis recta	Herbaceous clematis	Jun–Aug	sun	well-drained	1.5 m	90 cm
	Codonopsis clematidea	Codonopsis	Jun–Sep	sun/partial shade	well-drained	90 cm	climbing
	Crambe cordifolia	Seakale	Jun–Jul	sun	well-drained	1.8 m	1.8 m
	Crambe maritima	Seakale	Jun–Jul	sun	well-drained	60 cm	60 cm
	Dianthus 'Dad's Favourite'	Pink	Jun–Aug	sun	well-drained	30 cm	30 cm
	Dianthus 'Mrs Sinkins'	Pink	Jun–Aug	sun	well-drained	30 cm	30 cm
	Dictamnus albus	Burning bush	Jun–Aug	sun	well-drained	80 cm	60 cm
	Eremurus himalaicus	Foxtail lily	Jun–Jul	sun	well-drained	1.8 m	60 cm
	Erigeron 'Schneewittchen'	Fleabane	Jun–Aug	sun	well-drained	50 cm	45 cm
	Filipendula purpurea f. *albiflora*	Meadowsweet	Jun–Jul	partial shade	moist	90 cm	60 cm
	Galega × hartlandii 'Alba'	Goat's rue	Jun–Aug	sun	well-drained	1.5 m	90 cm
	Geranium clarkei 'Kashmir White'	Cranesbill	Jun–Aug	sun	well-drained	30 cm	45 cm
	Geranium macrorrhizum 'Album'	Cranesbill	Jun–Jul	shade	dry	25 cm	60 cm
	Gypsophila paniculata	Baby's breath	Jun–Aug	sun	well-drained	90 cm	90 cm
	Hemerocallis 'Gentle Shepherd'	Daylily	Jun–Aug	sun/partial shade	well-drained	90 cm	60 cm
	Iris 'Bianco'	Bearded iris	Jun–Jul	sun	well-drained	75 cm	30 cm
	Iris 'Bubbly Mood'	Bearded iris	Jun–Jul	sun	well-drained	75 cm	30 cm
	Iris ensata 'Snowdrift'	Japanese iris	Jun–Jul	sun	moist	80 cm	45 cm
	Iris sibirica 'White Swirl'	Siberian iris	Jun–Jul	sun	moist	90 cm	25 cm
	Lathryrus latifolius 'White Pearl'	Perennial pea	Jun–Aug	sun	well-drained	1.5 m	climbing
	Lilium candidum	Madonna lily	Jun–Jul	sun	well-drained	1.5 m	15 cm
	Lilium martagon var. *album*	Turkscap lily	Jun–Jul	partial shade/sun	well-drained	1.5 m	15 cm
	Linaria purpurea 'Springside White'	Toadflax	Jun–Aug	sun	well-drained/dry	90 cm	45 cm
	Lobelia erinus 'Snowball'	Lobelia	Jun–Oct	sun	well-drained	15 cm	15 cm
	Lobelia erinus 'White Fountain'	Lobelia	Jun–Oct	sun	well-drained	15 cm	trailing
	Lobularia maritima 'Carpet of Snow'	Alyssum	Jun–Oct	sun	well-drained	10 cm	25 cm
	Lychnis coronaria 'Alba'	Rose campion	Jun–Aug	sun	well-drained	60 cm	30 cm
	Lysimachia ephemerum	Loosestrife	Jun–Sep	sun	moist	1 m	30 cm
	Malva moschata f. *alba*	Musk mallow	Jun–Aug	sun	well-drained	75 cm	30 cm
	Nectaroscordum siculum	Nectaroscordum	May–Jun	sun/partial shade	well-drained/moist	1.2 m	30 cm
	Nemophila maculata	Fivespot	Jun–Aug	sun	well-drained/moist	15 cm	15 cm
	Paeonia lactiflora 'Whitleyi Major'	Peony	May–Jun	sun	well-drained/moist	85 cm	85 cm
	Papaver orientale 'Black and White'	Oriental poppy	May–Jun	sun	well-drained/dry	75 cm	60 cm
	Papaver orientale 'Picotee'	Oriental poppy	May–Jun	sun	well-drained/dry	75 cm	60 cm
	Pelargonium 'Beckwith Pink'	Zonal pelargonium	Jun–Oct	sun	well-drained	30 cm	30 cm
	Pelargonium 'Blanche Roche'	Ivy-leaved pelargonium	Jun–Oct	sun	well-drained	30 cm	trailing
	Pelargonium 'Maverick White'	Zonal geranium	Jun–Oct	sun	well-drained	30 cm	30 cm
	Petunia 'Surfinia White'	Trailing petunia	Jun–Oct	sun	well-drained	25 cm	trailing
	Petunia 'White Magic'	Grandiflora petunia	Jun–Oct	sun	well-drained	30 cm	30 cm
	Prunella grandiflora 'Alba'	Self-heal	Jun–Aug	sun/partial shade	moist	15 cm	45 cm
	Scabiosa caucasica 'Miss Willmott'	Scabious	Jun–Sep	sun	well-drained	60 cm	45 cm
	Sildacea candida	False mallow	Jun–Aug	sun/partial shade	well-drained	90 cm	45 cm

latin name	common name	flowering	sun/shade	moisture	height	spread
Viola cornuta 'Alba'	Viola	May–Aug	sun/partial shade	well-drained	15 cm	30 cm
Consolida ajacis 'Sydney Mixed'	Larkspur	Jun–Sep	sun	well-drained	90 cm	25 cm
Linaria maroccana 'Northern Lights'	Toad flax	Jun–Aug	sun	well-drained	60 cm	15 cm
Schizanthus pinnatus 'Angel Wings Mixed'	Poor man's orchid	Jun–Oct	sun	well-drained/moist	30 cm	25 cm
Tropaeolum majus 'Tip Top Mixed'	Nasturtium	Jun–Oct	sun	well-drained	25 cm	25 cm
Viola 'Irish Molly'	Viola	May–Aug	sun/partial shade	well-drained	15 cm	15 cm

summer: july

latin name	common name	flowering	sun/shade	moisture	height	spread
Allium sphaerocephalon	Ornamental onion	Jul–Aug	sun	well-drained	90 cm	10 cm
Clematis 'Madame Julia Correvon'	Clematis	Jul–Sep	sun	well-drained	1.8 m	spreading
Cosmos atrosanguineus p.77	Chocolate cosmos	Jul–Oct	sun	well-drained	80 cm	35 cm
Knautia macedonica p.70	Pincushion flower	Jul–Sep	sun	well-drained	45 cm	45 cm
Lilium 'Black Beauty'	Lily	Jul–Aug	sun	wel-drained	1 m	25 cm
Rosa 'Guinée'	Climbing rose	Jul–Aug	sun	moist/well-fed	5 m	climbing
Salpiglossis sinuata 'Chocolate Pot'	Salpiglossis	Jul–Oct	sun	well-drained/moist	60 cm	30 cm
Alstroemeria 'Mars'	Peruvian lily	Jul–Sep	sun	well-drained	1 m	30 cm
Amaranthus caudatus	Love lies bleeding	Jul–Oct	sun	well-drained/moist	1 m	60 cm
Astilbe × arendsii 'Fanal'	Astilbe	Jul–Aug	partial shade	wet	45 cm	30 cm
Begonia semperflorens 'Inferno Scarlet'	Begonia	Jul–Oct	sun/partial shade	well-drained	30 cm	30 cm
Begonia 'Zulu'	Begonia	Jul–Oct	sun	well-drained	45 cm	45 cm
Clematis 'Ernest Markham'	Clematis	Jul–Oct	sun	well-drained	3.6 m	spreading
Clematis 'Gravetye Beauty'	Clematis	Jul–Oct	sun	well-drained	1.8 m	spreading
Clematis 'Kermesina'	Clematis	Jul–Sep	sun	well-drained	3 m	spreading
Clematis 'Ville de Lyon'	Clematis	Jul–Oct	sun	well-drained	2.4 m	spreading
Cleome hassleriana 'Cherry Queen'	Spider flower	Jul–Sep	sun	well-drained	90 cm	45 cm
Crocosmia 'Lucifer'	Crocosmia	Jul–Sep	sun	well-drained	1 m	15 cm
Dianthus chinensis 'Chianti'	Indian pink	Jul–Oct	sun	well-drained	35 cm	20 cm
Dianthus superbus 'Crimsonia'	Pink	Jul–Oct	sun	well-drained	50 cm	25 cm
Hemerocallis 'Stafford'	Daylily	Jul–Sep	sun/partial shade	well-drained	90 cm	90 cm
Ipomoea lobata	Mina	Jul–Oct	sun	well-drained	1.8 m	climbing
Ismelia carinata 'German Flag'	Annual chrysanthemum	Jul–Sep	sun	well-drained	45 cm	30 cm
Kniphofia thomsonii	Red hot poker	Jul–Sep	sun/shelter	well-drained	1.2 m	30 cm
Lophospermum 'Red Dragon'	Twining snapdragon	Jul–Oct	sun	well-drained	1.8 m	climbing
Mimulus cardinalis	Monkey flower	Jul–Sep	sun/partial shade	moist	90 cm	40 cm
Penstemon barbatus	Penstemon	Jul–Oct	sun	well-drained	1.2 m	60 cm
Penstemon Garnet ('Andenken an Friedrich Hahn')	Penstemon	Jun–Oct	sun	well-drained	90 cm	60 cm
Phlox drummondii 'African Sunset'	Phlox	Jul–Sep	sun	well-drained	10 cm	20 cm
Potentilla atrosanguinea	Cinquefoil	Jun–Sep	sun	well-drained	45 cm	45 cm
Potentilla 'Gibson's Scarlet' p.68	Cinquefoil	Jun–Sep	sun	well-drained	60 cm	60 cm
Potentilla 'Monsieur Rouillard'	Cinquefoil	Jun–Sep	sun	well-drained	45 cm	45 cm
Salvia coccinea 'Lady in Red'	Salvia	Jul–Oct	sun	well-drained	40 cm	30 cm
Salvia splendens 'Blaze of Fire'	Salvia	Jul–Oct	sun	well-drained	30 cm	25 cm
Tropaeolum speciosum	Flame flower	Jul–Oct	partial shade	well-drained/moist	3 m	climbing
Zinnia elegans 'Dreamland Red'	Zinnia	Jul–Sep	sun	well-drained	25 cm	25 cm
Zinnia 'Red Spider'	Zinnia	Jul–Sep	sun	well-drained	45 cm	30 cm
Agastache 'Firebird'	Mexican hyssop	Jul–Sep	sun	well-drained	40 cm	25 cm
Alstroemeria 'Orange Gem'	Peruvian lily	Jul–Sep	sun	well-drained	1.5 m	45 cm
Brugmansia sanguinea	Angel's trumpet	Jul–Sep	sun	well-drained	1.2 m	90 cm
Gazania 'Orange Peacock'	Gazania	Jul–Oct	sun	well-drained	20 cm	20 cm
Ligularia dentata 'Desdemona'	Ligularia	Jul–Aug	sun	moist	1.2 m	90 cm
Ligularia dentata 'Othello'	Ligularia	Jul–Aug	sun	moist	1.2 m	90 cm
Lilium henryi	Lily	Jul–Aug	partial shade/sun	well-drained	1.2 m	15 cm
Mimulus 'Calypso'	Monkey flower	Jul–Sep	sun/partial shade	moist	15 cm	30 cm
Potentilla 'William Rollison'	Cinqufoil	Jun–Sep	sun	well-drained	60 cm	60 cm
Salvia splendens 'Orange Zest'	Salvia	Jul–Oct	sun	well-drained	30 cm	25 cm
Tithonia rotundifolia 'Goldfinger'	Mexican sunflower	Jul–Oct	sun	well-drained	75 cm	30 cm
Tropaeolum tuberosum 'Ken Aslet'	Climbing nasturtium	Jul–Oct	partial shade	well-drained	3 m	climbing
Zinnia elegans 'Desert Sun'	Zinnia	Jul–Sep	sun	well-drained	90 cm	40 cm
Zinnia haageana 'Persian Carpet'	Zinnia	Jul–Sep	sun	well-drained	40 cm	30 cm
Achillea 'Lachsschönheit'	Yarrow	Jul–Sep	sun	well-drained	60 cm	45 cm
Agastache 'Apricot Sprite'	Mexican hyssop	Jul–Sep	sun	well-drained	45 cm	30 cm
Alcea rosea 'Chater's Double Apricot'	Hollyhock	Jul–Sep	sun	moist	1.5 m	60 cm
Begonia sutherlandii	Begonia	Jul–Oct	sun	well-drained	20 cm	trailing
Crocosmia × crocosmiiflora 'Solfatare'	Crocosmia	Jul–Sep	sun	well-drained	60 cm	15 cm
Diascia berberae 'Blackthorn Apricot'	Diascia	Jul–Sep	sun	well-drained	45 cm	40 cm
Inula orientalis	Inula	Jul–Aug	sun	well-drained	60 cm	30 cm
Kniphofia 'Bees' Sunset'	Red hot poker	Jul–Sep	sun	well-drained	1 m	60 cm
Lilium African Queen Group	Lily	Jul–Aug	sun	well-drained	1.2 m	15 cm
Rudbekia hirta 'Marmalade'	Cone flower	Jul–Sep	sun	well-drained/moist	60 cm	30 cm
Achillea 'Moonshine'	Yarrow	Jul–Sep	sun	well-drained	60 cm	45 cm
Achillea filipendulina 'Gold Plate'	Yarrow	Jul–Sep	sun	well-drained	1.2 m	45 cm
Anthemis 'Grallach Gold'	Chamomile	Jul–Sep	sun	well-drained	60 cm	60 cm
Argemone mexicana	Prickly poppy	Jul–Sep	sun	dry	1 m	40 cm
Begonia 'Primrose'	Begonia	Jul–Oct	sun	well-drained	45 cm	45 cm
Bidens ferulifolia	Bidens	Jul–Oct	sun	well-drained	45 cm	spreading
Cautleya spicata 'Robusta'	Cautleya	Jul–Sep	partial shade	moist	60 cm	30 cm
Clematis rehderiana	Clematis	Jul–Oct	sun	well-drained	3 m	spreading
Coreopsis verticillata 'Zagreb'	Tickseed	Jul–Sep	sun	well-drained	35 cm	30 cm
Crocosmia × crocosmiiflora 'Citronella'	Crocosmia	Jul–Sep	sun	well-drained	60 cm	15 cm
Datura 'Double Golden Queen'	Angel's trumpet	Jul–Sep	sun	well-drained	1.5 m	90 cm
Filipendula ulmaria 'Aurea'	Golden meadowsweet	Jul–Aug	partial shade	moist	60 cm	45 cm

Gazania 'Daybreak Red Stripe'	Gazania	Jul–Oct	sun	well-drained	25 cm	25 cm
Helianthus 'Capenoch Star'	Perennial sunflower	Jul–Sep	sun	well-drained	1.2 m	60 cm
Hemerocallis citrina p.80	Daylily	Jul–Aug	sun/partial shade	well-drained	70 cm	60 cm
Inula hookeri	Inula	Jul–Aug	sun	well-drained	75 cm	60 cm
Inula magnifica	Inula	Jul–Aug	sun	well-drained	1.8 m	60 cm
Ipomoea lobata 'Citronella'	Mina	Jul–Oct	sun	well-drained	1.8 m	climbing
Lathyrus chloranthus	Sweet pea	Jul–Sep	sun	well-drained	1.5 m	climbing
Ligularia przewalskii	Ligularia	Jul–Aug	sun	moist	2 m	60 cm
Lilium Citronella Group	Turkscap lily	Jul–Aug	partial shade	well-drained	1.2 m	15 cm
Lilium 'Connecticut King'	Lily	Jul–Aug	sun	well-drained	1 m	15 cm
Origanum vulgare 'Aureum'	Golden marjoram	Jul–Oct	sun	well-drained	8 cm	spreading
Phlomis russeliana	Jerusalem sage	Jun–Aug	sun	well-drained	90 cm	60 cm
Rosa 'Mermaid'	Climbing rose	Jun–Oct	sun/partial shade	moist/well-fed	10 cm	climbing
Rudbekia hirta 'Goldilocks'	Cone flower	Jul–Sep	sun	well-drained/moist	60 cm	30 cm
Thalictrum flavum subsp. *glaucum*	Meadow rue	Jul–Sep	sun/partial shade	well-drained/moist	1.2 m	60 cm
Verbascum bombyciferum	Mullein	Jul–Sep	sun	well-drained	1.8 m	60 cm
Verbascum 'Cotswold Queen'	Mullein	Jul–Sep	sun	well-drained	1.2 m	30 cm
Verbascum 'Gainsborough'	Mullein	Jul–Sep	sun	well-drained	1 m	30 cm
Verbascum olympicum	Mullein	Jul–Sep	sun	well-drained	1.8 m	60 cm
Alcea rosea 'Chater's Double Soft Yellow'	Hollyhock	Jul–Sep	sun	moist	2.4 m	60 cm
***Anthemis tinctoria* 'Sauce Hollandaise'** p.69	Chamomile	Jul–Sep	sun	well-drained	90 cm	90 cm
Coreopsis verticillata 'Moonbeam'	Tickseed	Jul–Sep	sun	well-drained	40 cm	30 cm
Leucanthemum × *superbum* 'Sonnenschein'	Shasta daisy	Jul–Aug	sun	well-drained	90 cm	30 cm
Mimulus naiandinus 'Andean Nymph'	Monkey flower	Jul–Sep	sun	moist	15 cm	15 cm
Osteospermum 'Buttermilk'	Cape daisy	Jul–Oct	sun	well-drained	60 cm	60 cm
Xanthophthalmum coronarium 'Primrose Gem'	Annual chrysanthemum	Jul–Sep	sun	well-drained	45 cm	30 cm
Galtonia princeps	Summer hyacinth	Jul–Aug	sun	well-drained	45 cm	25 cm
Galtonia viridiflora	Summer hyacinth	Jul–Aug	sun	well-drained	60 cm	25 cm
Nicotiana langsdorffii	Tobacco plant	Jul–Oct	partial shade/sun	well-drained	1.2 m	45 cm
Nicotiana 'Lime Green'	Tobacco plant	Jul–Oct	partial shade/sun	well-drained	60 cm	30 cm
Convolvulus tricolor 'Royal Ensign'	Dwarf morning glory	Jul–Sep	sun	well-drained	30 cm	30 cm
Salpiglossis sinuata 'Blue Peacock'	Salpiglossis	Jul–Oct	sun	well-drained/moist	60 cm	30 cm
Agastache foeniculum	Mexican hyssop	Jul–Sep	sun	well-drained	90 cm	45 cm
Anchusa azurea 'Blue Angel'	Anchusa	Jul–Sep	sun	well-drained	20 cm	15 cm
Brachyscome iberidifolia 'Blue Star'	Swan river daisy	Jul–Sep	sun	well-drained	30 cm	30 cm
Browallia speciosa 'Blue Troll'	Bush violet	Jul-Sep	sun	well-drained	25 cm	25 cm
Catananche caerulea	Cupid's dart	Jul–Aug	sun	well-drained	60 cm	30 cm
Cynoglossum amabile 'Blue Shower'	Chinese forget-me-not	Jul–Sep	sun/partial shade	well-drained	40 cm	30 cm
Echinops bannaticus 'Taplow Blue'	Globe thistle	Jul–Sep	sun	dry	2m	60 cm
Echinops ritro 'Veitch's Blue'	Globe thistle	Jul–Sep	sun	dry	1 .2m	60 cm
Eryngium agavifolium	Sea holly	Jul–Sep	sun	well-drained	1.5 m	60 cm
Geranium wallichianum 'Buxton's Variety'	Cranesbill	Jul–Oct	sun	well-drained	30 cm	90 cm
Lathyrus sativus	Chickling pea	Jul–Sep	sun	well-drained	1.2 m	climbing
Lupinus mutabilis var. *cruckshankii* 'Sunrise'	Annual lupin	Jul–Oct	sun	well-drained	90 cm	30 cm
Lupinus texensis	Blue bonnet	Jul–Sep	sun	well-drained	45 cm	25 cm
Nolana paradoxa 'Bluebird'	Nolana	Jul–Sep	sun	well-drained	15 cm	15 cm
Perovskia 'Blue Spire'	Russian sage	Jul–Oct	sun	well-drained	90 cm	60 cm
Phlox drummondii 'Bobby Sox'	Phlox	Jul–Sep	sun	well-drained	20 cm	20 cm
Platycodon grandiflorus 'Mariesii'	Balloon flower	Jun–Aug	sun/partial shade	moist	40 cm	45 cm
Salvia farinacea 'Victoria'	Salvia	Jul–Oct	sun	well-drained	60 cm	30 cm
Salvia transsylvanica	Salvia	Jul–Sep	sun	well-drained	60 cm	30 cm
Aconitum × *cammarum* 'Bicolor'	Monkshood	Jul–Aug	partial shade	moist	1.2 m	45 cm
Clematis 'Perle d'Azur'	Clematis	Jul–Sep	sun	well-drained	3 m	spreading
Lathyrus nervosus	Lord Anson's pea	Jul–Sep	sun	well-drained	1.8 m	climbing
Trachymene caerulea	Didiscus	Jul–Sep	sun	well-drained	60 cm	30 cm
Achillea millefolium 'Cerise Queen'	Yarrow	Jul–Sep	sun	well-drained	60 cm	40 cm
Clematis 'Duchess of Albany'	Clematis	Jul–Oct	sun	well-drained	1.8 m	spreading
Diascia barberae 'Ruby Field'	Diascia	Jul–Sep	sun	well-drained	45 cm	40 cm
***Geranium* 'Ann Folkard'** p.72	Cranesbill	Jun–Sep	sun	well-drained	30 cm	spreading
Geranium psilostemon	Cranesbill	Jun–Sep	sun	well-drained	90 cm	90 cm
Geranium riversleaiaum 'Russell Prichard'	Cranesbill	Jun–Sep	sun	well-drained	15 cm	45 cm
Lablab purpureus	Indian bean	Jul–Sep	sun	well-drained	3 m	climbing
***Lathyrus odoratus* 'Painted Lady'** p.71	Sweet pea	Jun–Sep	sun	well-drained	1.8 m	climbing
Lilium Pink Perfection Group	Lily	Jul–Aug	partial shade	well-drained	1.5 cm	30 cm
Lupinus aridus 'Summer Spires'	Annual lupin	Jul–Sep	sun	well-drained	90 cm	30 cm
Lychnis coronaria	Rose campion	Jun–Aug	sun	well-drained	60 cm	30 cm
Lythrum salicaria Firecandle ('Feuerkerze')	Purple loosestrife	Jul–Sep	sun/partial shade	moist	1.2 m	45 cm
Malope trifida 'Tetra Vulcan'	Mallow	Jul–Sep	sun	well-drained	60 cm	25 cm
Maurandya 'Victoria Falls'	Twining snapdragon	Jul–Oct	sun	well-drained	15 cm	trailing
Xeranthemum annuum	Xeranthemum	Jul–Sep	sun	well-drained	60 cm	45 cm
Alstroemeria ligtu hybrids	Peruvian lily	Jul–Sep	sun	well-drained	80 cm	30 cm
Astilbe chinensis	Astilbe	Jul–Aug	partial shade	wet	1.8 m	50 cm
Astilbe 'Sprite'	Astilbe	Jul–Aug	partial shade	wet	25 cm	30 cm
Begonia 'Lady Rowena'	Begonia	Jul–Oct	sun	well-drained	45 cm	45 cm
Begonia semperflorens 'Pink Sundae'	Begonia	Jul–Oct	sun/partial shade	well-drained	20 cm	20 cm
Chelone obliqua	Turtle head	Jul–Sep	sun	well-drained	80 cm	45 cm
Convolvulus althaeoides	Convolvulus	Jul–Sep	sun	dry	1.8 m	climbing
Crinum × *powellii*	Crinum	Jul–Sep	sun	well-drained	90 cm	90 cm
Dianthus chinensis 'Baby Doll Mixed'	Indian pink	Jul–Oct	sun	well-drained	15 cm	15 cm
Dierama pulcherrimum	Fairy's wand	Jul–Aug	sun	well-drained/moist	1.5 m	30 cm
Eremurus 'Harmony'	Foxtail lily	Jul–Sep	sun	well-drained	1.5 m	60 cm
Gaura lindheimeri 'Siskiyou Pink'	Gaura	Jul–Sep	sun	well-drained	1 m	90 cm
Gazania 'Rose Kiss'	Gazania	Jul–Oct	sun	well-drained	20 cm	20 cm
Lavatera trimestris 'Silver Cup'	Mallow	Jul–Sep	sun	well-drained	60 cm	45 cm
Lilium 'Stargazer'	Lily	Jul–Aug	sun	well-drained	1 m	15 cm
Lychnis coronaria Oculata Group	Rose campion	Jun–Aug	sun	well-drained	90 cm	30 cm
Lythrum salicaria 'Lady Sackville'	Purple loosestrife	Jul–Sep	sun/partial shade	moist	75 cm	45 cm

Origanum vulgare 'Country Cream'	Oregano	Jul–Oct	sun	well-drained	30 cm	30 cm
Pelargonium 'Grey Lady Plymouth'	Scented-leafed pelargonium	Jul–Oct	sun	well-drained	60 cm	35 cm
Phlomis tuberosa	Jerusalem sage	Jun–Aug	sun	well-drained	90 cm	60 cm
Phlox drummondii 'Chanel'	Phlox	Jul–Sep	sun	well-drained	20 cm	20 cm
Phuopsis stylosa	Phuopsis	Jun–Aug	sun	well-drained	25 cm	60 cm
Salvia coccinea 'Cherry Blossom'	Salvia	Jul–Oct	sun	well-drained	40 cm	30 cm
Silene caroliniana 'Hot Pink'	Catchfly	Jul–Oct	sun	well-drained	15 cm	10 cm
Verbascum 'Pink Domino'	Mullein	Jul–Sep	sun	well-drained	1 m	30 cm
Amberboa moschata	Sweet sultan	Jul–Sep	sun	well-drained	45 cm	20 cm
Clarkia unguiculata 'Apple Blossom'	Clarkia	Jul–Sep	sun	well-drained	90 cm	20 cm
Diascia rigescens p.81	Diascia	Jul–Sep	sun	well-drained	45 cm	40 cm
Lythrum salicaria 'Blush'	Purple loosestrife	Jul–Sep	sun/partial shade	moist	75 cm	45 cm
Macleaya microcarpa 'Coral Plume'	Plume poppy	Jul–Sep	sun/partial shade	well-drained	2 m	90 cm
Nicotiana 'Havana Apple Blossom'	Tobacco plant	Jul–Oct	partial shade/sun	well-drained	35 cm	20 cm
Pelargonium 'Chocolate Peppermint'	Scented-leafed pelargonium	Jul–Oct	sun	well-drained	45 cm	45 cm
Pelargonium 'Mabel Grey'	Scented-leafed pelargonium	Jul–Oct	sun	well-drained	60 cm	60 cm
Penstemon 'Apple Blossom'	Penstemon	Jun–Oct	sun	well-drained	60 cm	60 cm
Rosa 'Gloire de Dijon'	Climbing rose	Jun–Aug	sun/partial shade	moist/well-fed	5 m	climbing
Rosa 'New Dawn'	Climbing rose	Jun–Sep	sun	moist/well-fed	3 m	climbing
Silene coeli-rosa 'Cherry Blossom'	Viscaria	Jul–Oct	sun	well-drained	60 cm	15 cm
Acanthus mollis	Bear's breeches	Jul–Sep	sun	well-drained	1.2 m	60 cm
Acanthus spinosus	Bear's breeches	Jul–Sep	sun	well-drained	1.2 m	60 cm
Alcea rosea 'Nigra' p.78	Hollyhock	Jul–Sep	sun	moist	2.4 m	60 cm
Amaranthus 'Intense Purple'	Love lies bleeding	Jul–Oct	sun	well-drained/moist	1 m	60 cm
Brachyscome iberidifolia 'Purple Splendour'	Swan river daisy	Jul–Sep	sun	well-drained	30 cm	30 cm
Clematis 'Empress of India'	Clematis	Jul–Aug	sun	well-drained	2.4 m	spreading
Clematis 'Etoile Violette' p.74	Clematis	Jul–Sep	sun	well-drained	2.4 m	spreading
Clematis 'Royal Velours'	Clematis	Jul–Sep	sun	well-drained	3 m	spreading
Clematis 'Venosa Violacea'	Clematis	Jul–Sep	sun	well-drained	2.4 m	spreading
Clematis 'Warsawska Nike'	Clematis	Jul–Sep	sun	well-drained	2.4 m	spreading
Clematis viticella 'Purpurea plena elegans'	Clematis	Jul–Sep	sun	well-drained	3 m	spreading
Cobaea scandens	Cathedral bells	Jul–Oct	sun	well-drained/moist	3 m	climbing
Lathyrus odoratus 'Matucana'	Sweet pea	Jul–Sep	sun	well-drained	1.8 m	climbing
Lythrum virgatum 'Dropmore Purple'	Purple loosestrife	Jul–Sep	sun/partial shade	moist	1.2 m	45 cm
Origanum laevigatum 'Herrenhausen'	Oregano	Jul–Oct	sun	well-drained	60 cm	30 cm
Penstemon 'Blackbird' p.71	Penstemon	Jun–Oct	sun	well-drained	90 cm	60 cm
Roscoea auriculata	Roscoea	Jul–Aug	partial shade	moist	40 cm	15 cm
Salvia × *superba*	Sage	Jun–Aug	sun	well-drained	90 cm	45 cm
Scabiosa atropurpurea 'Ace of Spades'	Pincushion flower	Jul–Sep	sun	well-drained	60 cm	30 cm
Cleome hassleriana 'Violet Queen'	Spider flower	Jul–Sep	sun	well-drained	90 cm	45 cm
Datura metel 'Cornucopaea'	Angel's trumpet	Jul–Sep	sun	well-drained	1.5 m	90 cm
Diascia 'Lilac Belle'	Diascia	Jul–Sep	sun	well-drained	10 cm	10 cm
Heliotropium 'Marine'	Cherry pie	Jul–Sep	sun	well-drained/moist	45 cm	30 cm
Liatris spicata	Gay feather	Jun–Aug	sun	well-drained/moist	60 cm	25 cm
Penstemon 'Sour Grapes'	Penstemon	Jun–Oct	sun	well-drained	90 cm	60 cm
Penstemon 'Stapleford Gem'	Penstemon	Jun–Oct	sun	well-drained	75 cm	60 cm
Thalictrum delavayi 'Hewitt's Double'	Meadow rue	Jul–Sep	sun/partial shade	well-drained/moist	1.5 m	60 cm
Eryngium giganteum p.79	Miss Willmott's ghost	Jul–Sep	sun	well-drained	1 m	60 cm
Onopordum acanthium	Scotch thistle	Jul–Sep	sun	well-drained	3 m	1 m
Achillea ptarmica 'The Pearl'	Yarrow	Jul–Sep	sun	well-drained	60 cm	45 cm
Aconitum napellus subsp. *vulgare* 'Albidum'	Monkshood	Jul–Aug	partial shade	moist	90 cm	30 cm
Actaea racemosa	Bugbane	Jul–Aug	sun/partial shade	moist	1.8 m	60 cm
Alstroemeria 'Apollo'	Peruvian lily	Jul–Sep	sun	well-drained	1 m	30 cm
Althaea officinalis alba	Marsh mallow	Jul–Sep	sun	moist	1.8 m	60 cm
Argemone grandiflora	Prickly poppy	Jul–Sep	sun	dry	1.2 m	40 cm
Astilbe 'Professor van der Wielen'	Astilbe	Jul–Aug	partial shade	wet	1 m	45 cm
Begonia 'Billie Langdon'	Begonia	Jul–Oct	sun	well-drained	45 cm	45 cm
Brachyscome iberidifolia 'White Splendour'	Swan river daisy	Jul–Sep	sun	well-drained	30 cm	30 cm
Brugmansia suaveolens	Angel's trumpet	Jul–Sep	sun	well-drained	2.5 m	90 cm
Cardiocrinum giganteum	Cardiocrinum	Jul–Sep	partial shade	moist	3 m	1 m
Catananche caerulea 'Bicolor'	Cupid's dart	Jul–Aug	sun	well-drained	60 cm	30 cm
Clarkia pulchella 'Snowflake'	Clarkia	Jul–Sep	sun	well-drained	45 cm	20 cm
Clematis 'Alba Luxurians'	Clematis	Jul–Sep	sun	well-drained	3 m	spreading
Clematis recta 'Purpurea'	Herbaceous clematis	Jul–Aug	sun	well-drained	1.2 m	90 cm
Cleome hassleriana 'Helen Campbell'	Spider flower	Jul–Sep	sun	well-drained	90 cm	45 cm
Cobaea scandens f. *alba*	Cathedral bells	Jul–Oct	sun	well-drained/moist	3 m	climbing
Crinum × *powellii* 'Album'	Crinum	Jul–Sep	sun	well-drained	90 cm	90 cm
Epilobium angustifolium var. *album*	Rosebay willowherb	Jun–Aug	sun	well-drained	2 m	40 cm
Galtonia candicans p.73	Summer hyacinth	Jul–Aug	sun	well-drained	75 cm	25 cm
Gaura lindheimeri	Gaura	Jul–Sep	sun	well-drained	1 m	90 cm
Gypsophila elegans 'Covent Garden'	Baby's breath	Jul–Sep	sun	well-drained	60 cm	30 cm
Lavatera trimestris 'Mont Blanc'	Mallow	Jul–Sep	sun	well-drained	50 cm	45 cm
Leucanthemum × *superbum* 'Wirral Supreme'	Shasta daisy	Jul–Aug	sun	well-drained	90 cm	30 cm
Lilium 'Casa Blanca'	Lily	Jul–Aug	sun	well-drained	1.2 m	15 cm
Lilium longiflorum	Easter lily	Jul–Aug	partial shade	well-drained	90 cm	15 cm
Lilium regale p.75	Regal lily	Jul–Aug	sun	well-drained	1.5 m	15 cm
Lupinus hartwegii 'Biancaneve'	Annual lupin	Jul–Sep	sun	well-drained	90 cm	30 cm
Nicotiana 'Domino White'	Tobacco plant	Jul–Oct	partial shade/sun	well-drained	30 cm	15 cm
Nicotiana × *sanderae* 'Fragrant Cloud'	Tobacco plant	Jul–Oct	partial shade/sun	well-drained	90 cm	30 cm
Osteospermum 'Whirligig'	Cape daisy	Jul–Oct	sun	well-drained	60 cm	60 cm
Pelargonium tomentosum	Species pelargonium	Jul–Oct	sun/partial shade	well-drained	60 cm	60 cm
Penstemon digitalis 'Husker Red'	Penstemon	Jun–Oct	sun	well-drained	1 m	60 cm
Penstemon 'White Bedder'	Penstemon	Jun–Oct	sun	well-drained	70 cm	60 cm
Physostegia virginiana 'Summer Snow'	Obedient plant	Jul–Sep	sun	moist	70 cm	60 cm
Salvia farinacea 'Alba'	Salvia	Jul–Oct	sun	well-drained	60 cm	30 cm
Salvia sclarea var. *turkestanica alba*	Biennial clary	Jul–Sep	sun	well-drained	1 m	30 cm
Verbascum chaixii 'Album' p.76	Mullein	Jul–Sep	sun	well-drained	90 cm	30 cm

latin name	common name	flowering	sun/shade	moisture	height	spread
Veronicastrum virginicum album	Speedwell	Jul–Sep	sun	well-drained/moist	1.2 m	45 cm
Zantedeschia aethiopica 'Crowborough'	Calla lily	Jul–Sep	sun	moist	45 cm	45 cm
Mirabilis jalapa	Four o'clock flower	Jul–Sep	sun	well-drained	60 cm	60 cm
Salvia viridis	Annual clary sage	Jul–Sep	sun	well-drained	45 cm	30 cm

summer: august

latin name	common name	flowering	sun/shade	moisture	height	spread
Lobelia 'Queen Victoria'	Lobelia	Aug–Oct	partial shade/sun	moist	90 cm	30 cm
Sedum telephium 'Munstead Red'	Stonecrop	Aug–Oct	sun	well-drained/dry	60 cm	60 cm
Cosmos sulphureus 'Ladybird Mixed'	Cosmos	Aug–Oct	sun	well-drained	25 cm	15 cm
Ipomoea × sloteri	Cardinal climber	Aug–Oct	sun	well-drained/moist	1.5 m	climbing
Kniphofia 'Alcazar'	Red hot poker	Aug–Oct	sun	well-drained	90 cm	60 cm
Monarda 'Cambridge Scarlet' p.93	Bergamot	Jul–Sep	sun/partial shade	moist/well-drained	90 cm	45 cm
Ricinus communis 'Carmencita'	Castor oil plant	Aug–Oct	sun	well-drained/moist	1.8 m	90 cm
Cosmos sulphureus 'Polidor''	Cosmos	Aug–Oct	sun	well-drained	90 cm	30 cm
Helenium 'Coppelia'	Sneezeweed	Aug–Sep	sun	well-drained/moist	1 m	45 cm
Helenium 'Moerheim Beauty' p.88	Sneezeweed	Jul–Aug	sun	well-drained/moist	1 m	45 cm
Kniphofia 'Shining Sceptre'	Red hot poker	Aug–Sep	sun	well-drained	90 cm	60 cm
Leonotis leonurus	Leonotis	Aug–Sep	sun	well-drained	1.5 cm	60 cm
Cerinthe major	Honeywort	Aug–Oct	sun	well-drained	60 cm	45 cm
Cerinthe minor 'Bouquet Gold'	Honeywort	Aug–Oct	sun	well-drained	45 cm	30 cm
Helenium 'Butterpat'	Sneezeweed	Aug–Sep	sun	well-drained/moist	1 m	45 cm
Kirengeshoma palmata	Kirengeshoma	Jul–Sep	partial shade	moist	90 cm	60 cm
Kniphofia 'Little Maid' p.94	Red hot poker	Aug–Oct	sun	well-drained	45 cm	25 cm
Eucomis bicolor p.95	Pineapple flower	Aug–Sep	sun	well-drained	45 cm	45 cm
Eucomis comosa	Pineapple flower	Aug–Sep	sun	well-drained	60 cm	45 cm
Kniphofia 'Percy's Pride'	Red hot poker	Aug–Oct	sun	well-drained	1 m	60 cm
Molucella laevis	Bells of Ireland	Aug–Oct	sun	well-drained/moist	60 cm	20 cm
Aconitum 'Spark's Variety'	Monkshood	Aug–Sep	partial shade	moist	1 m	45 cm
Agapanthus p.84	Lily of the Nile	Aug–Sep	sun	well-drained	75 cm	30 cm
Agapanthus africanus	Lily of the Nile	Aug–Sep	sun	well-drained	75 cm	30 cm
Agapanthus campanulatus	Lily of the Nile	Aug–Sep	sun	well-drained	60 cm	30 cm
Gentiana asclepiadea	Willow gentian	Aug–Oct	partial shade	moist	60 cm	60 cm
Ipomoea tricolor 'Heavenly Blue' p.90	Morning glory	Aug–Oct	sun	well-drained/moist	1.8 m	climbing
Lobelia siphilitica	Lobelia	Aug–Oct	sun	moist	60 cm	30 cm
Clematis heracleifolia	Herbaceous clematis	Aug–Sep	sun	well-drained	1.5 m	spreading
Lilium speciosum var. rubrum	Lily	Aug–Sep	partial shade	moist	1.2 m	15 cm
Phlox maculata 'Alpha'	Phlox	Jul–Sep	sun/partial shade	well-drained/moist	90 cm	45 cm
Rosa 'Zéphirine Drouhin'	Climbing rose	Jun–Sep	sun/partial shade	moist/well-fed	2.7 m	climbing
Agastache mexicana	Mexican hyssop	Aug–Sep	sun	well-drained	60 cm	30 cm
Cosmos bipinnatus 'Versailles Tetra'	Cosmos	Aug–Oct	sun	well-drained	90 cm	30 cm
Monarda 'Croftway Pink'	Bergamot	Jul–Sep	sun/partial shade	moist/well-drained	90 cm	45 cm
Physotegia virginiana 'Vivid'	Obedient plant	Aug–Oct	sun	moist	50 cm	45 cm
Sedum spectabile 'Brilliant'	Stonecrop	Aug–Oct	sun	well-drained/dry	30 cm	30 cm
Iberis umbellata 'Appleblossom'	Candytuft	Aug–Oct	sun	well-drained	15 cm	10 cm
Phlox paniculata 'Mother of Pearl'	Phlox	Jul–Sep	sun/partial shade	well-drained/moist	1.2 m	45 cm
Angelica gigas p.92	Angelica	Aug–Oct	sun	moist	1.2 m	60 cm
Cerinthe major 'Purpurascens' p.89	Honeywort	Aug–Oct	sun	well-drained	45 cm	30 cm
Clematis 'Gipsy Queen'	Clematis	Aug–Oct	sun	well-drained	3.6 m	spreading
Ipomoea purpurea	Morning glory	Aug–Oct	sun	well-drained/moist	1.8 m	climbing
Lobelia × gerardii 'Vedrariensis'	Lobelia	Aug–Oct	partial shade/sun	moist	1.2 m	30 cm
Monarda 'Prärienacht'	Bergamot	Jul–Sep	sun/partial shade	moist/well-drained	90 cm	45 cm
Sedum maximum 'Atropurpureum'	Stonecrop	Aug–Oct	sun	well-drained/dry	60 cm	60 cm
Limonium platyphyllum (latifolium)	Sea lavender	Jul–Sep	sun	well-drained/dry	45 cm	45 cm
Monarda 'Aquarius'	Bergamot	Jul–Sep	sun/partial shade	moist/well-drained	90 cm	45 cm
Phlox maculata 'Rosalinde'	Phlox	Jul–Sep	sun/partial shade	well-drained/moist	90 cm	45 cm
Phlox paniculata p.85	Phlox	Jul–Sep	sun/partial shade	well-drained/moist	1.2 m	45 cm
Phlox paniculata 'Prospero'	Phlox	Jul–Sep	sun/partial shade	well-drained/moist	1.2 m	45 cm
Tricyrtis formosana	Toad lily	Aug–Oct	sun/partial shade	moist	60 cm	45 cm
Verbena bonariensis p.87	Purple top	Jun–Oct	sun	well-drained	1.5 m	45 cm
Actaea simplex Atropurpurea Group	Bugbane	Aug–Sep	sun/partial shade	moist	2.1 m	60 cm
Agapanthus campanulatus var. albidus	Lily of the Nile	Aug–Sep	sun	well-drained	90 cm	45 cm
Cosmos bipinnatus 'Sonata White'	Cosmos	Aug–Oct	sun	well-drained	1.2 m	30 cm
Iberis crenata	Candytuft	Aug–Oct	sun	well-drained	30 cm	20 cm
Lysimachia clethroides	Gooseneck loosestrife	Aug–Oct	sun/partial shade	moist	1 m	60 cm
Macleaya cordata	Plume poppy	Aug–Sep	sun/partial shade	well-drained	1.8 m	60 cm
Monarda 'Schneewittchen'	Bergamot	Jul–Sep	sun/partial shade	moist/well-drained	90 cm	45 cm
Nicotiana sylvestris p.91	Tobacco plant	Jul–Oct	partial shade/sun	well-drained	1.5 m	60 cm
Phlox maculata 'Omega'	Phlox	Jul–Sep	sun/partial shade	well-drained/moist	90 cm	45 cm
Romneya coulteri p.86	California tree poppy	Jul–Oct	sun	well-drained/dry	2 m	90 cm
Rosa 'Margaret Merril'	Rose	Jun–Sep	sun	moist	75 cm	75 cm
Iberis umbellata 'Fairy Mixed'	Candytuft	Aug–Oct	sun	well-drained	20 cm	15 cm

autumn: september

latin name	common name	flowering	sun/shade	moisture	height	spread
Dahlia 'Arabian Night'	Dahlia	Aug–Oct	sun	well-drained/moist	1.2 m	60 cm
Helianthus 'Velvet Queen' p.98	Annual sunflower	Aug–Sept	sun	well-drained	1.5 m	45 cm

	latin name	common name	flowering	sun/shade	moisture	height	spread
	Clematis cirrhosa var. balearica	Clematis	Jan–Mar	sun	well-drained	5 m	spreading
	Clematis cirrhosa 'Freckles' p.118	Clematis	Jan–Mar	sun	well-drained	5 m	spreading
	Clematis cirrhosa 'Wisley Cream'	Clematis	Jan–Mar	sun	well-drained	5 m	spreading
	Helleborus argutifolius p.119	Corsican hellebore	Jan–Mar	partial shade	moist	60 cm	60 cm
	Helleborus foetidus	Stinking hellebore	Dec–Mar	partial shade	moist	45 cm	45 cm
	Helleborus foetidus Wester Flisk Group	Stinking hellebore	Dec–Mar	partial shade	moist	45 cm	45 cm
	Helleborus lividus	Hellebore	Dec–Mar	partial shade/shelter	moist	45 cm	30 cm
	Cyclamen coum p.123	Cyclamen	Jan–Mar	shade	moist	10 cm	10 cm
	Iris unguicularis 'Mary Barnard' p.120	Iris	Dec–Jan	sun	dry	30 cm	30 cm
	Iris unguicularis 'Walter Butt'	Iris	Dec–Jan	sun	dry	30 cm	30 cm
	Cyclamen coum f. pallidum 'Album'	Cyclamen	Jan–Mar	shade	moist	10 cm	10 cm
	Cyclamen coum 'Maurice Dryden'	Cyclamen	Jan–Mar	shade	moist	10 cm	10 cm
	Helleborus niger	Christmas rose	Dec–Mar	partial shade	moist	30 cm	45 cm
	Helleborus × nigercors	Hellebore	Jan–Mar	partial shade	moist	35 cm	35 cm

winter: february

	latin name	common name	flowering	sun/shade	moisture	height	spread
	Camellia japonica 'Adolphe Audusson'	Camellia	Feb–Mar	partial shade	well-drained/acid	5 m	3 m
	Camellia sasanqua 'Crimson King'	Camellia	Feb–Mar	partial shade	well-drained/acid	3 m	1.5 m
	Crocus 'Gypsy Girl'	Crocus	Feb–Mar	sun	well-drained	7 cm	3 cm
	Eranthis cilicica	Winter aconite	Feb–Mar	partial shade	moist	10 cm	8 cm
	Narcissus 'February Gold'	Daffodil	Feb–Mar	sun	well-drained	30 cm	8 cm
	Narcissus 'Jumblie'	Daffodil	Feb–Mar	sun	well-drained	17 cm	8 cm
	Narcissus 'Tête-à-tête'	Daffodil	Feb–Mar	sun	well-drained	15 cm	5 cm
	Crocus 'Cream Beauty'	Crocus	Feb–Mar	sun	well-drained	7 cm	3 cm
	Helleborus cyclophyllus	Hellebore	Feb–Apr	partial shade	moist	40 cm	40 cm
	Helleborus viridis	Hellebore	Feb–Apr	partial shade	moist	40 cm	40 cm
	Iris reticulata	Iris	Feb–Mar	sun	well-drained	15 cm	5 cm
	Hepatica × media 'Harvington Beauty'	Hepatica	Feb–Mar	partial shade	well-drained	15 cm	20 cm
	Iris histrioides 'Major'	Iris	Jan–Feb	sun	well-drained	10 cm	5 cm
	Crocus 'Blue Pearl'	Crocus	Feb–Mar	sun	well-drained	7 cm	3 cm
	Iris 'Katharine Hodgkin' p.128	Iris	Feb–Mar	sun	well-drained	10 cm	5 cm
	Camellia × williamsii 'Debbie' p.126	Camellia	Feb–Mar	partial shade	well-drained/acid	4 m	2.5 m
	Camellia × williamsii 'Donation'	Camellia	Feb–Mar	partial shade	well-drained/acid	4 m	2.5 m
	Camellia × williamsii 'J.C. Williams'	Camellia	Feb–Mar	partial shade	well-drained/acid	4 m	2.5 m
	Crocus tommasinianus 'Whitewell Purple' p.127	Crocus	Feb–Mar	sun	well-drained	7 cm	3 cm
	Iris 'J.S. Dijt'	Iris	Feb–Mar	sun	well-drained	10 cm	5 cm
	Crocus etruscus 'Zwanenburg'	Crocus	Feb–Mar	sun	well-drained	7 cm	3 cm
	Camellia 'Cornish Snow'	Camellia	Feb–Mar	partial shade	well-drained/acid	4 m	2.5 m
	Camellia japonica 'Alba Simplex'	Camellia	Feb–Mar	partial shade	well-drained/acid	4 m	2.5 m
	Crocus biflorus subsp. alexandri	Crocus	Feb–Mar	sun	well-drained	7 cm	3 cm
	Crocus 'Snow Bunting'	Crocus	Feb–Mar	sun	well-drained	7 cm	3 cm
	Galanthus 'Atkinsii'	Snowdrop	Feb–Mar	partial shade	moist	15 cm	10 cm
	Galanthus elwesii	Snowdrop	Feb–Mar	partial shade	moist	15 cm	10 cm
	Galanthus nivalis	Snowdrop	Feb–Mar	partial shade	moist	15 cm	10 cm
	Galanthus nivalis 'Flore Pleno'	Snowdrop	Feb–Mar	partial shade	moist	15 cm	10 cm
	Galanthus 'S. Arnott' p.131	Snowdrop	Feb–Mar	partial shade	moist	15 cm	10 cm
	Leucojum vernum	Spring snowflake	Feb–Mar	partial shade	moist	15 cm	10 cm
	Helleborus orientalis hybrids p.129	Lenten rose	Feb–Apr	partial shade	moist	45 cm	45 cm
	Hepatica nobilis	Hepatica	Feb–Mar	partial shade	moist	10 cm	20 cm
	Hepatica nobilis var. japonica	Hepatica	Feb–Mar	partial shade	moist	10 cm	20 cm
	Hepatica transsilvanica p.130	Hepatica	Feb–Mar	partial shade	moist	10 cm	20 cm

Index of Featured Plants

calendar of flowering plants & index

latin name	common name	flowering	sun/shade	moisture	height	spread
Canna indica 'Purpurea'	Indian shot	Jul–Oct	sun	moist	2 m	60 cm
Dahlia 'Bishop of Llandaff' p.105	Dahlia	Aug–Oct	sun	well-drained/moist	1.2 m	60 cm
Lobelia tupa	Lobelia	Sept–Oct	sun/shelter	well-drained	1.8 m	60 cm
Canna 'Assaut'	Canna	Jul–Oct	sun	moist	1.2 m	60 cm
Canna 'Durban'	Canna	Jul–Oct	sun	moist	1 m	60 cm
Canna 'Wyoming' p.101	Canna	Jul–Oct	sun	moist	2 m	60 cm
Crocosmia × crocosmiiflora 'Emily McKenzie' p.99	Crocosmia	Aug–Oct	sun	well-drained	50 cm	15 cm
Crocosmia × crocosmiiflora 'Star of the East'	Crocosmia	Aug–Oct	sun	well-drained	90 cm	15 cm
Dahlia 'David Howard'	Dahlia	Aug–Oct	sun	well-drained/moist	1.5 m	60 cm
Dahlia 'Ellen Houston'	Dahlia	Aug–Oct	sun	well-drained/moist	75 cm	45 cm
Kniphofia rooperi	Red hot poker	Sept–Oct	sun	well-drained	1.2m	60 cm
Clematis 'Bill McKenzie'	Clematis	Jul–Oct	sun	well-drained	4.5 m	spreading
Clematis tangutica	Clematis	Jul–Oct	sun	well-drained	4.5 m	spreading
Dahlia 'Clair de Lune'	Dahlia	Aug–Oct	sun	well-drained/moist	1.2m	60 cm
Helianthus salicifolius	Perennial sunflower	Sept–Oct	sun	well-drained	2 m	60 cm
Rudbekia fulgida var. *sullivantii* 'Goldsturm'	Coneflower	Jul–Oct	sun	well-drained/moist	75 cm	30 cm
Helianthus 'Lemon Queen'	Perennial sunflower	Sept–Oct	sun	well-drained	2 m	60 cm
Helianthus 'Moonwalker'	Annual sunflower	Aug–Sept	sun	well-drained	1.5m	45 cm
Helianthus 'Italian White'	Annual sunflower	Aug–Sept	sun	well-drained	1.5 m	45 cm
Ceratostigma plumbaginoides	Hardy plumbago	Aug–Oct	sun	well-drained	30 cm	30 cm
Salvia patens p.103	Gentian sage	Aug–Oct	sun	well-drained	60 cm	45 cm
Calamintha nepeta 'Blue Cloud'	Calamint	Aug–Oct	sun	well-drained	50 cm	45 cm
Salvia uliginosa	Bog sage	Sept–Nov	sun	moist	2 m	45 cm
Anemone hupehensis 'Hadspen Abundance'	Japanese anemone	Sept–Oct	partial shade	well-drained	90 cm	30 cm
Sedum 'Autumn Joy' p.100	Stonecrop	Sept–Nov	sun	well-drained/dry	45 cm	45 cm
Anemone × hybrida 'September Charm'	Japanese anemone	Sept–Oct	partial shade	well-drained	40 cm	30 cm
Colchicum 'The Giant'	Meadow saffron	Sept–Oct	sun	well-drained	20 cm	5 cm
Colchicum cilicicum 'Purpureum'	Meadow saffron	Sept–Oct	sun	well-drained	15 cm	5 cm
Echinacea purpurea p.107	Coneflower	Jul–Oct	sun	well-drained	90 cm	40 cm
Eupatorium purpureum 'Atropurpureum'	Joe pye weed	Aug–Oct	sun	moist	1.8 m	90 cm
Clematis × jouiniana 'Praecox'	Herbaceous clematis	Sep–Oct	sun	well-drained	1.8 m	spreading
Clematis 'Lady Betty Balfour'	Clematis	Sept–Oct	sun	well-drained	3.6 m	spreading
Colchicum autumnale p.106	Meadow saffron	Sept–Oct	sun	well-drained	10 cm	5 cm
Dahlia merckii	Dahlia	Aug–Oct	sun	well-drained/moist	2 m	60 cm
Actaea matsumurae 'White Pearl'	Bugbane	Sept–Oct	sun/partial shade	moist	1.2 m	60 cm
Anemone × hybrida 'Honorine Jobert' p.104	Japanese anemone	Sept–Oct	partial shade	well-drained	90 cm	30 cm
Clematis flammula	Clematis	Aug–Oct	sun	well-drained	7 m	spreading
Colchicum autumnale 'Album'	Meadow saffron	Sept–Oct	sun	well-drained	10 cm	5 cm
Colchicum speciosum 'Album'	Meadow saffron	Sept–Oct	sun	well-drained	15 cm	5 cm
Echinacea purpurea 'White Swan'	Coneflower	Jul–Oct	sun	well-drained	90 cm	40 cm
Eucomis autumnalis	Pineapple flower	Sept–Oct	sun	well-drained	45 cm	45 cm
Gladiolus callianthus p.102	Gladiolus	Aug–Sept	sun	well-drained	90 cm	20 cm

autumn: october & november

latin name	common name	flowering	sun/shade	moisture	height	spread
Chrysanthemum 'Bullfinch'	Chrysanthemum	Sep–Nov	sun	well-drained/moist	60 cm	45 cm
Iris foetidissima	Gladdon	Oct–Dec	shade	dry	60 cm	45 cm
Nerine 'Red Pimpernel'	Guernsey lily	Oct–Nov	sun/shelter	well-drained	45 cm	15 cm
Rosa moyesii p.114	Rose	Jun–Sep	sun/partial shade	moist	2 m	1.8 m
Schizostylis coccinea p.111	Crimson flag	Sept–Nov	sun	moist	60 cm	25 cm
Chrysanthemum 'Mary Stoker'	Chrysanthemum	Sep–Nov	sun	well-drained/moist	60 cm	45 cm
Chrysanthemum 'Nantyderry Sunshine'	Chrysanthemum	Sep–Nov	sun	well-drained/moist	75 cm	40 cm
Aconitum carmichaelii 'Arendsii' p.110	Monkshood	Sept–Oct	partial shade	moist	1.8 m	30 cm
Salvia guaranitica 'Blue Enigma'	Salvia	Aug–Oct	sun	well-drained	1.5 m	60 cm
Chrysanthemum 'Emperor of China' p.115	Chrysanthemum	Sep–Nov	sun	well-drained/moist	1.2 m	60 cm
Aster novi-belgii 'Patricia Ballard'	Aster	Sep–Oct	sun	well-drained	75 cm	40 cm
Chrysanthemum 'Mei-kyo'	Chrysanthemum	Sep–Nov	sun	well-drained/moist	75 cm	60 cm
Cyclamen cilicium	Cyclamen	Oct–Nov	shade	moist	10 cm	10 cm
Cyclamen hederifolium p.112	Cyclamen	Oct–Nov	shade	moist	10 cm	10 cm
Nerine bowdenii p.113	Guernsey lily	Oct–Nov	sun	well-drained	45 cm	15 cm
Schizostylis coccinea 'Miss Hegarty'	Crimson flag	Sept–Nov	sun	moist	60 cm	25 cm
Aster amellus 'King George'	Aster	Sept–Oct	sun	well-drained	60 cm	45 cm
Aster amellus 'Veilchenkoenigin'	Aster	Sept–Oct	sun	well-drained	60 cm	45 cm
Aster × frikartii 'Mönch' p.115	Aster	Sept–Oct	sun	well-drained	75 cm	40 cm
Crocus sativus	Saffron crocus	Oct–Nov	sun	well-drained	7 cm	3 cm
Crocus speciosus	Autumn crocus	Oct–Nov	sun	well-drained	15 cm	4 cm
Liriope muscari	Lilyturf	Sept–Nov	partial shade/sun	moist	30 cm	30 cm
Aster diviracatus	Aster	Sept–Oct	sun	well-drained	60 cm	45 cm
Aster ericoides	Aster	Sept–Oct	sun	well-drained	90 cm	30 cm
Crocus ochroleucus	Autumn crocus	Oct–Nov	sun	well-drained	12 cm	4 cm
Cyclamen hederifolium f. *albiflorum*	Cyclamen	Oct–Nov	shade	moist		

winter: december & january

latin name	common name	flowering	sun/shade	moisture	height	spread
Adonis amurensis p.122	Adonis	Jan–Mar	sun	moist	15 cm	25 cm
Eranthis hyemalis p.121	Winter aconite	Jan–Feb	partial shade	moist	10 cm	8 cm
Iris danfordiae	Iris	Jan–Feb	sun	well-drained	10 cm	5 cm